TALENT MANAGEMENT

Published by:
Tilak Wasan
DISCOVERY PUBLISHING HOUSE PVT. LTD
4383/4B, Ansari Road, Darya Ganj
New Delhi-110 002 (India)
Phone : +91-11-23279245, 43596064-65
Fax : +91-11-23253475
E-mail : parul.wasan@gmail.com
discoverypublishinghouse@gmail.com
web : www.discoverypublishinggroup.c

First Edition: 2013

ISBN: 978-93-5056-307-6

Talent Management

Printed at:
Dynamic Printers
Delhi

TALENT MANAGEMENT

TALENT MANAGEMENT

Edited by

Dr. Rabi Narayana Misra

M.Com., LL.B.

DPH

DISCOVERY PUBLISHING HOUSE PVT. LTD.

NEW DELHI-110 002

Published by:
Tilak Wasan
DISCOVERY PUBLISHING HOUSE PVT. LTD.
4383/4B, Ansari Road, Darya Ganj
New Delhi-110 002 (India)
Phone : +91-11-23279245, 43596064-65
Fax : +91-11-23253475
E-mail : parul.wasan@gmail.com
discoverypublishinghouse@gmail.com
web : www.discoverypublishinggroup.com

***First Edition:* 2013**

ISBN: 978-93-5056-307-6

Talent Management

Printed at:
Dynamic Printers
Delhi

Preface

Talent management is the implementation of integrated strategies or systems designed to increase workforce productivity by developing improved processes and proper utilizing people with the required skills and aptitude to meet current and future business needs. Talent management implies recognizing a person's inherent skills, traits, personality and offering him a matching job. Every person has a unique talent that suits a particular job profile and any other position will cause discomfort. Talent management is beneficial to both the organization and employees. It creates better linkage between individuals' efforts and business goals.

In this globalized world it is only the Human Resource that can provide an organization competitive edge, because under the new trade agreements, technology can be easily transferred from one country to another. Now we need talented workforce for overall development of the organization. This book is very essential for Management Students, H.R. Managers and to the research scholars and Government undertaking for proper utilization of their work-force to increase production and productivity.

Dr Rabi N. Misra

Acknowledgement

I am very much thankful to all paper contributors of this book. It is not possible in my part to edit this book without their help and co-operation.

My special thanks to my wife Smt. Swarna Prava Misra for her kind co-operation and encouragement for editing this book. I am also thanking to both of my sons Roopesh and Rookesh for their help in editing this book. My elder daughter in law Smt. Amrita Rani Misra and younger daughter in law Smt. Bandita Misra have also given their timely help to edit this book.

Last but not least, a special word of thanks to Mr. Tilak Wasan, the Owner/Director of Discovery Publishing House (P) Ltd, New Delhi for publishing this book in time. I also place on record my sincere thanks to his son who is the real man for doing all publication works. Finally, I would like to thanks all members of publication division of Discovery Publishing House for their help and co-operation for publishing the book in time.

Dr Rabi N. Misra

Contents

CHAPTER

1

Talent Management

—*Mr. Santanu Kumar Das**

Infosys, Wipro, Satyam, HCL Technologies and i-Flex Solutions. These are some of the companies, which have the highest revenue growth rates year after year. Few of them also have revenues exceeding $1 bn. They provide great work environment to their people.

Good salary, perks, overseas assignments, challenging and highly competitive work environment and a great future—these are some of the pluses associated with these companies. Then, can these companies be considered as the picture perfect companies with no problems whatsoever?

Think again!!!

Have a Look at these Figures

- Infosys-10.7 per cent
- Wipro-17 per cent
- Satyam-18 per cent

*Mr. Das, Faculty Member, Sri Vivakananda Institute of Management, Berhampur-3, Orissa.

- HCL Technologies-13.1 per cent
- i-Flex Solutions-19 per cent
- These are the attrition rates of the employees of the above mentioned companies. Some of these actually match their revenue growth rates!!! This is giving a severe headache to the top management in general and HR department in particular. So, this has added to the functions of the HR department a new function—Talent Management.

Introduction

- Talent management implies recognizing a person's inherent skills, traits, personality and offering him a matching job. Every person has a unique talent that suits a particular job profile and any other position will cause discomfort. It is the job of the Management, particularly the HR Department, to place candidates with prudence and caution. A wrong fit will result in further hiring, re-training and other wasteful activities.
- Talent Management is beneficial to both the organization and the employees. The organization benefits from: Increased productivity and capability; a better linkage between individuals' efforts and business goals; commitment of valued employees; reduced turnover; increased bench strength and a better fit between people's jobs and skills. Employees benefit from: Higher motivation and commitment; career development; increased knowledge about and contribution to company goals; sustained motivation and job satisfaction.
- In these days of highly competitive world, where change is the only constant factor, it is important for an organization to develop the most important resource of all—the Human Resource. In this globalized world, it is only the Human Resource that can provide an organization the competitive edge because under the

new trade agreements, technology can be easily transferred from one country to another and there is no dearth for sources of cheap finance. But it is the talented workforce that is very hard to find. The biggest problem is how to retain the present workforce and stop them from quitting?

Importance

First, let us look at some of the reasons for the importance of talent management.

- **Globalization:** Now for any jobseeker the whole world is the potential place to find employment. One can know the opportunities available in any part of the world easily and the number of talent seekers has also increased.
- **Increased Competition:** Increased competition in the market place has necessitated the need for consistently good performance on the side of organizations. These have made the companies to put in all efforts to hire and retain the best talent in the respective field of operation.
- **Increasing Knowledge:** The knowledge era has necessitated the retaining of those talents which have the ability to assimilate new technologies and knowledge, which are growing at a pace never seen before.
- **The Challenge:** The challenge of talent management has two facets to it. First is how to find new people and second is how to retain the present workforce. Each of the challenges has to be tackled in the most efficient way possible so that the organization can achieve its objectives.

The First Challenge—Where to Find New Talent?

All the organizations are finding loads of business opportunities and consequently, their revenues are growing at a rapid pace. The increasing business opportunities has necessitated that these organizations go in for massive recruitment. But, the question is where to find the best talent which is able to fit the job description and also adjust to the organization's values and norms. If we scan the environment, we find there is a shortage of skilled workforce that can be employed.

Some of the possible reasons that have led to the shortage are:

1. **Demographic Constraints:** This is a common problem faced by many of the developed countries, where a large chunk of its population is nearing the age of retirement or is over 50 years. USA, Germany and Japan are facing the same problem. All these countries will see a decline in their workforce and talent. In the coming years, they will see a great shortage in their skilled professionals.
2. **Existing Educational System:** The graduates and the postgraduates that are being churned out of the universities are found to be ill-equipped to handle the challenges of the workplace. They are mostly equipped with only the theoretical aspects of the issues and lack the application part. The educational system is faulty and does not take industry needs into consideration, resulting in a mismatch between industry requirements and educational preparation.
3. **Cost Factor:** Recruiting new employees is becoming tougher and tougher in the developing countries, where the HR Department has to sort out thousands of applications for $ handful of jobs. Finding right person for the right job becomes a very difficult process. It also involves very high cost to conduct the recruitment and selection process for such a large population of applicants.
4. **Attracting the Best Talent:** This is another challenge. As was the case in the past, the best available talent is

not just motivated by the name and fame of the organization. Not any more. They have a new set of motivators like—challenging work, conducive work a environment and freedom from bureaucratic structure.

The Second Challenge—How to Retain the Existing Employees?

- Gone are the days when a person would join an organization in his mid-20s and would work till his retirement in the late-50s. Today the young professionals hop jobs, especially during the first 4-5 years of their work life.
- Though the Indian service industry is basking in the light of outsourced jobs from the developed countries, they also cannot ignore the fact that the BPO industry is also facing one of the highest attrition rates, in fact never heard before in India, of around 35 per cent.
- It is a fact that its the people that add value to organizations. It is also a fact that humans are a restless species who, unlike the immovable Banyan Tree, cannot stay rooted in one place. People need to move on for one reason or another, and the organization stands to lose. Let us look at some of the reasons behind the massive attrition rates:
- Gap between organizational values and goals and the personal values and goals is one of the major reasons of the attrition rates. If they go parallel, there is no way both would be satisfied and inevitably, the organization would lose out on a talented employee.
- Working environment is another major factor. Employees in the knowledge era demand creative and a democratic work environment. Failure on the part of the management to provide such an environment will result in a talented employee leaving the organization.

- The competitive world has made sure that there is high work pressure on the employees of any organization. This has led to psychological problems like stress, and in extreme situations, total burnouts. It also leads to other health related problems.
- Movement for higher salary is also common among the younger professionals. There is no shortage for organizations who are looking for talented employees and who are ready to shell out a hefty salary for a talented person. Other lures like better job opportunities, higher posts and overseas assignments are also major factors in the attrition rates.
- Not taking proper care during the recruitment and selection process and not taking proper care to fit the right person to the right job also breeds dissatisfaction among the employees.
- Bad or opaque policies from management on issues of succession planning and promotion, appointments for senior positions also is a major factor which makes the organization lose out on the talented employees.
- The professionals have different aspirations at different times of their career. During the initial years, they have good salary and foreign assignments. Next on the list is working on cutting edge technology. More seasoned professionals look for learning opportunities. So employees tend to move to those organizations which provide them with means to fulfil their aspirations.
- **Good Working Environment:** It has to be accepted by the organizations that highly talented persons make their own rules. They have to be provided with a democratic and a stimulating work environment. The organizational rules must be flexible enough to provide them with freedom to carry out their part of task to their liking, as long as the task is achieved. Opportunities should also be provided to the employees to achieve their personal goals.

- Retaining the present employees is of the foremost importance to the organizations because; the company would have already incurred heavy costs in the form of training and development. Now if the organization has to look for a replacement for the employee who has left, it involves a lot of costs like - hiring costs, training costs and the induction costs.
- Also it takes some time for the new employee to adjust to the new work environment. During this time the productivity of the employee will be low. The HR department will have to fit the new employee into a proper role in the organization. Apart from causing the company a monetary loss and breaks in their day-to-day operations, attrition contributes to knowledge transfer, which is a great loss and adversely affects business.

The Question is—How to Manage the TALENT?

- It is now proved beyond doubt that, in the era of technology and knowledge, talent is in the driving seat. One who possesses it dictates. Not he who pays for it. It is the demand of the time that business leaders elevate management of talent to a burning corporate priority. It is not a walk in the park for the talent market. Quality people are no longer available in plenty, easily replaceable and relatively inexpensive.
- These are some of the measures that should be taken into account to hire and retain talent in the organization, to be efficient and competitive in this highly competitive world:
- **Hire the Right People:** Proper care must be taken while hiring the people itself. It would be beneficial for an organization to recruit young people and nurture them, than to substitute by hiring from other organizations. Questions to be asked at this stage are: Whether the person has the requisite skills needed for

the job? Whether the person's values and goals match with those of organization's? In short, care must be taken to fit the right person to the right job.

- **Keep the Promises:** Good talent cannot be motivated by fake platitudes, half-truths and broken promises. Unfulfilled expectations can breed dissatisfaction among the employees and make them either leave the organization or work below their productive level. Promises made during the hiring stage must be kept to build loyalty among the employees, so that they are satisfied and work to their fullest capability.
- **Recognition of Merit:** It is highly motivating for any person if his talent is recognized and is suitably rewarded. One way is providing them with salary commensurate with their performance. Promotions and incentives based on performance are another way of doing it. Another way is by providing them with challenging projects. This will achieve two objectives - it makes employee feel that he is considered important (a highly motivating factor) and gets the work done in a efficient manner and brings out the best in the employee.
- **Providing Learning Opportunities:** Employees must be provided with continuous learning opportunities on and off work field through management development programmes and distance learning programmes. This will also benefit the organization in the form of highly talented workforce.
- **Shielding from High Work Pressure:** If an organization has to make the most of the available talent, they should be provided with adequate time to relax, so that they can di-stress themselves. It is very important to provide them with holidays and all-expenses-paid trips, so that they can come back refreshed to work and with increased energy. They must also be encouraged

to pursue their interests which are also a good way of reducing work environment stress. Recreation clubs, entertain programmes, fun activities with in the work area will also reduce the work life stress of the employees and develop camaraderie among the workers and result in a good working environment.

Conclusion

Highly demanding business environment makes it imperative for the organizations to build competence in the form of superior intellectual capital. It is agreed by almost all CEOs of big companies that it is the human resource—a talented one—that can provide them competitiveness in the long run. So it is the duty of the HR department to nurture a brigade of talented workforce, which can win them the war in the business field. The talent has to be spotted, carefully nurtured and most importantly preserved.

- **Right person for the right job—is the new mantra of Talent Management.**

CHAPTER

2

Talent Management
Driver for Organizational Success

*—P. Subramanyam**

Introduction

"It is nearly unanimous that HR can and should add more value to corporations. The best way to do this is by being a business partner—by directly improving the performance of the business. This can be accomplished by effective talent management, helping with change management/influencing strategy and a host of other value-added activities that impact effectiveness."

In a competitive marketplace, talent management is a primary driver for organizational success. Broadly defined, talent management is the implementation of integrated strategies or systems designed to increase workplace productivity by developing improved processes for attracting, developing, retaining and utilizing people with the required skills and aptitude to meet current and future business needs. A recent study shows that 85 per cent of HR executives state that the "single greatest challenge in workforce management

*Lecturer in Commerce, Govt. College (A) Rajahmundry, A.P.

is creating or maintaining their companies' ability to compete for talent." Without question, effective talent management provides one of the most critical points of strategic leverage today.

Offering enormous business value, talent management is complex and continually evolving. Influenced by external factors such as the economy, global expansion and mergers and acquisitions, critical success factors for effective talent management include alignment with strategic goals, active CEO participation and HR management. Over time, common themes around talent management are emerging, such as the role of line leaders in the development of talent. Overall, the main recurring themes are CEO involvement, culture, management, processes and accountability.

Research shows that organizations increasingly focus on talent management. Moving from reactive to proactive, companies are working hard to harness talent. According to SHRM's 2006 Talent Management Survey Report, 53 per cent of organizations have specific talent management initiatives in place. Of these companies, 76 per cent consider talent management a top priority. In addition, 85 per cent of HR professionals in these companies work directly with management to implement talent management strategies.

Yet, different companies may not define talent the same way. The belief in talent and its impact on the bottom line are at the heart of talent management. To be effective, the talent mindset must be embedded throughout the organization, starting with the CEO. Going beyond succession planning for top leadership positions, companies that value talent have a deep appreciation for the contribution of individuals at all levels, now and for the future. In essence, talent is the vehicle to move the organization where it wants to be.

Drivers for Talent Management

To gain competitive advantage, the demand for human capital drives talent management. Talent management strategies focus on five primary areas: attracting/ selecting, engaging, developing and retaining employees. Although pay and benefits initially attract employees, top-tier leadership organizations focus on retaining and developing talent.

Workforce trends drive talent management strategies. Factors such as an increasingly global and virtual workforce, different generations working together, longer life expectancies and an empowered and autonomous workforce have forever changed the workplace. Due to demographic changes, the workforce is also increasingly diverse—from age, gender and ethnicity to lifestyles, migration patterns and cultural norms. Organizations are already taking advantage of these workplace trends. For example, The Home Depot, Inc., the home improvement giant, focuses its staffing initiatives on older workers and partners with AARP for referrals; 15 per cent of its workforce is over 50. Talent management strategies also provide the context for diversity and inclusion. Proctor and Gamble, for example, feels that getting the right mix of people is a major part of talent management and hires many of its leaders as university recruits.

Talent management is also driven by the anticipated skills shortage in the coming years. While not all organizations, industries and professions will experience a lack of skills, organizations are already competing for talent. For example, customer service, health care, computer support and technology repair are areas where there is an anticipated acute talents shortage. In addition, as noted in SHRM's 2005 Future of the U.S. Labour Pool Survey Report, the anticipated loss of talent in the next decade will vary by organization size, sector and industry. For example, large organizations—as compared with small and medium companies—are more concerned about loss of talent from the retirement of the baby boom generation, and public and government organizations are more concerned about the loss of potential talent than private companies.

Finally, key business strategies also drive talent management. For example, with the growing need for global technical expertise, Ford Motor Company links competency development to its organizational strategic goals. Corporate branding, a key organizational strategy, is another business strategy that drives talent management. Increasingly, firms are linking their brand to employees and corporate behaviour. At JP Morgan Chase, for example, the concept of leadership for all employees is part of its corporate branding: "One Firm, One Team, Be a Leader."

Ownership of Talent Management

Supported by the CEO and the board of directors, talent management is headed by human resources, usually the head of the HR organization (*e.g.*, vice president of HR, chief human resource officer). While responsibility for talent management is shared throughout the organization—from the CEO to the line manager—the role of HR is to identify and deploy optimal strategies to engage employees by driving satisfaction, loyalty and retention. Commitment to talent management requires HR to be a strategic business partner. A 2005 study on global human capital found that chief HR officers (CHROs), as "chief talent architects," played a central role as strategic business advisors by leveraging human capital to improve organizational performance and workforce effectiveness. Based on CEO priorities, the top seven CHRO initiatives were organization transformation, people development, talent management, HR transformation, leadership development, recruitment initiatives and rewards.

Moving talent management initiatives forward, however, requires organizational buy-in. That is, all levels of management must be on board with the importance of talent management strategies. When the board is involved, the value of talent management is apparent and has high visibility. Yet to be successful, the value must be understood throughout the organization. In high-performing companies, for example, senior management also is responsible for the success of talent management. At the same time, for talent management initiatives to be effective, organizations need formal processes, with many people involved and with strong links between leadership and talent to translate into specific organizational value-based behaviours.

Ownership of talent management is also reflected in dedicated resources. A formal budget for talent management initiatives, for example, is evidence of organizational commitment. As noted in SHRM's 2006 Talent Management Survey Report, firms with talent management initiatives are more likely than organizations without such initiatives to have formal recruitment budgets (72% compared with 39%, respectively).

Further, it is important that HR educate top management on the link between the talent management cycle and the cost of turnover. For example, an employee's decision to stay or leave is related to career possibilities in the company as well as how he or she can become better prepared to move to other opportunities. To keep a valued employee, the easy answer is not merely compensation. Employee loyalty tends to be more directed to his or her professional skills rather than to the organization. Thus, to best attract, engage, develop and retain talent, those who have responsibility for talent management must understand what is important to employees.

CHAPTER

3

Building an Integrated Talent Management Strategy

—*K. Navina**

—*Dr. R.N. Misra***

Introduction

Senior executives often claim that people drive the value of the business. They are right. According to a recent survey conducted by the Economist Intelligence Unit for Oracle, senior executives at corporations worldwide judge the ability to attract and retain people as one of the most critical enablers of growth. But they have to be the right people. Every organisation relies on key clusters of critical talent in order to be able to execute its business strategy. These employees drive a disproportionate share of revenue and earnings. They generate high value for customers and shareholders. They have strong skills and deep knowledge—not just of the work itself, but of how to make things happen in the organisation. Without such employees, senior executives would be "pushing on a string" rather than executing their strategies.

*Lecturer in Commerce Govt. Degree College, Narsannapeta, Srikakulam District, A.P.

**Dr. R.N. Misra, Professor SMIT Berhampur, Orissa.

> *The ability to attract and retain people is one of the most critical enablers of growth.*

Moreover, the skills and knowledge of such employees ensure that they are in great demand. They are valuable to their current employers. They may be even more valuable to their current employer's competitors. Without a talent management strategy focused on keeping critical people engaged—including talent maps, targeted training, clear career paths, job rotation and other development tools—critical employees may be sending out resume's rather than executing the organisation's strategy.

Developing a Talent Management Strategy

The task of developing a talent management strategy often falls to human resources (HR) professionals working in consultation with the business functions. But HR also carries out the more traditional administrative functions such as handling employee benefits, delivering payrolls, ensuring compliance with government regulations, and recruiting and interviewing new staff. To become truly value-added partners in any business, HR needs the resources, tools and management buy-in to get the administrative tasks under control and move up to a position of strategic adviser. From talent mapping and planning to performance evaluation, recruitment, retention and even benefits administration, today's human capital professionals are constantly seeking new ways to streamline, integrate and align human capital functions with broader corporate objectives.

Mary Massung is an HR-focused executive at Unisys Corporation and vice-president of Unisys University, an in-house training and development vehicle. She is among those who claim that it is people who create the value in an enterprise: "That's especially true in a service business like ours, where you're not just selling your company; you're selling the skills and abilities of your people. If your people don't have the right skills to meet the expectations of your clients, your organisation will fail."

According to Ms Massung, the management team at Unisys Corporation "very much understands the strategic value of human resources". In fact, she says, business managers at the company "very much view us in HR as a strategic partner—someone they can turn to help them achieve their business goals".

"If your people don't have the right skills to meet the expectations of your clients, your organisation will fail."

Unisys Corporation is not alone. Anecdotal evidence indicates that more and more management teams are waking up to the value of a more deliberate approach to managing people and talent. This is the case at a large European bank. According to the firm's senior vice-president of HR, as the company began to measure its employee engagement, it made an interesting discovery. "What we began to notice", says the executive, "was that almost every measure of performance success we were to observe, be it profit margin or customer satisfaction, moved almost in lockstep with indices of employee satisfaction."

That realisation led the organisation to additional findings. "What we learned was that the more attention you pay to individual employees, the greater their satisfaction," says the executive. This is not to say simply pay the workers more and increase their benefits. Instead, explains the executive, "it's often simply taking an interest. Ask them how they like their work/life balance? Do they feel challenged or valued in their work? Are they satisfied with where they are? Are they aware of development opportunities and advancement?"

These are simple questions, but there is enormous value in developing a consistent means of gathering, analysing and responding to the answers. Essentially, says the executive, "we're helping our people plan and manage their careers. We're taking an interest in their personal development, and satisfaction." Treating people as individuals and addressing their strengths, weaknesses, and work and life goals "has an enormous impact on people's attitudes towards their work". The executive believes that this, in turn, "translates into stronger performance and higher retention".

A senior financial executive of a large US technology firm agrees, adding that one of the ways his HR executives deliver value is by helping the company to customise the careers of its most valuable workers. "We call it a life plan," he says. "Where do they want to go in the organisation? What do they want in their life?" By going through the process of designing and continually updating an individual career path, he says, "we get more from our people, and we keep them longer".

Both the bank and the technology firm are elevating the HR function from a primarily administrative focus to a more strategic one. Says the technology executive: "You may need to treat people as individuals, but you need to manage your people-focused processes collectively, based on facts. Only in this way "can you maximise the value of your workforce. You can turn people management into a competitive differentiator, a source of advantage."

Perhaps the key step that the technology firm has taken is to communicate to managers throughout the company that they will be measured by—and to some degree compensated on—the degree to which their employees are engaged. Simply put, engagement is a key driver of performance. And by monitoring and measuring engagement, the human resources function can provide critical insight to managers on what works, what doesn't, and how they can do better.

The Importance of Integration

The technology executive believes that herein also lies the importance of having an integrated and consistent technology platform for human resources management. "To be effective in human capital management today, you need very precise and timely information about individuals—and you also need to be able to analyse this information collectively in order to make informed decisions." The more integration between activities as diverse as recruitment, payroll and benefits management, training/development and performance measurement, "the better you'll be at overall workforce planning, the better you'll be at managing and motivating individual workers, and so the more effective you'll become as an organisation".

An integrated technology platform also gives HR executives more time to focus on strategic issues. Says the banking executive: "We're a dynamic organisation where people move around a Lot." So whether a manager or employee is in London, Prague, Dublin or elsewhere, "the performance management system, the frameworks and the software are all consistent". This enables the company to create "one culture" and "one set of processes". It also "enables HR to spend less time on administration and more time on value-adding activities".

At its most basic level, organisations deploy HR software to reduce the burden of day-to-day administrative tasks such as payroll or benefits reporting and compliance. Adding self-service HR administration not only reduces costs, but generally increases employees' sense of control and their satisfaction. As JoAnne Moeller, vice-president of human resources, compensation, benefits and HR-Information management for Office Depot, explains, "automating routine HR tasks significantly reduces costs". But at the same time, the HR clients "like do-it-yourself HR services because they can get what they need from wherever they are and whenever they want".

But HR technology can also help to execute more value-added tasks. For example, in the case of talent management, technology can help organisations to implement improvements in the following areas:

> *Integrated HR processes can tie together employee performance, evaluation and compensation—from the executive suite to the machine shop.*

- ***Recruitment***: Is the organisation pursuing the right people? How successful is it in attracting the right candidates? Tools such as e-recruitment or onsite application kiosks are a start. The results can be gathered and analysed to generate benchmarks. And randomised trials can help organisations to track the effectiveness of competing recruiting techniques.
- ***Talent Mapping***: Given the organisation's business focus and strategic direction, what mix of talent and skills will help it to execute successfully? If the talent mix is absent, how can it be developed or acquired? Working with line and senior management, HR executives can develop recruiting strategies and design training programmes that focus on existing or emerging needs.
- ***Workforce Planning and Development***: Much of the work of the HR function focuses on getting the organisation's human capital from its current state (where it is now) to some future state (where it needs to be). These efforts can be documented and tracked by:
  - creating detailed workforce planning and skills gap assessments;
  - identifying high-potential personnel (and following through with additional development and retention services); and
  - adopting more flexible development programmes and reaching a broader audience through e-learning.
- ***Performance Planning and Evaluation***: Employees who understand where they add value do a better job of adding value. And managers who clearly communi-

cate what they expect from their employees, and how these expectations tie into compensation, help employees become more engaged and effective. Here, HR systems can help managers to develop feedback loops between performance expectations and actual performance over time, evaluate the effectiveness of performance metrics, enable a range of review techniques and create a single home for all information about an individual employee.

You need to have an idea of what you want to accomplish for your business and the ways better management of people can help you achieve that".

In short, integrated HR processes can tie together employee performance, evaluation and compensation from the executive suite to the machine shop, research and development (R&D) lab, warehouse or sales floor. These processes clearly link the value people create to how people are valued. For instance, at Costco, inventory shrinkage—the reduction in inventory value through shoplifting or employee theft; damaged, stale or lost products; or paperwork errors—is controlled by tying one-fifth of the bonus of all employees to this metric.

- ***Retention:*** Retention is another area where consistent processes can help the HR function to identify clusters of key talent, set retention bench-marks, apply retention strategies, and then evaluate and refine approaches over time. For example, clear and broadly implemented processes can help companies to:
  - determine the characteristics that best define the most critical performers, then proactively manage their development, compensation and engagement over time;
  - identify the early warning signs of employee defection, in time to act;

- evaluate the degree to which various combinations of incentives influence behaviour and retention, and establish an optimal budget for rewards; and
- establish a formal learning and development plan for all employees and track progress by individuals or groups of "like" employees.

Strategy First

Technology-enabled processes may be powerful. But strategy comes first, says Lars Mørch, a member of Danske Bank's executive committee and the head of the group's HR function. Danske Bank is the largest bank in Denmark and one of the largest in Scandinavia, with total assets of over US $500 bn.

"You need to have an idea of what you want to accomplish for your business and the ways better management of people can help you achieve that," explains Mr Mørch. But once a company knows what it wants to accomplish in HR, "that's when you can determine what technology you need—and then the technology becomes a tool to help you achieve your strategy".

Danske Bank: Growth takes Talent

Close alignment between HR and business strategies is "always important", states Lars Mørch, a member of Danske Bank's executive committee and the head of the group's HR function. But having HR strategies that march to the same beat as those of senior and line management is even more important when an organisation is pursuing significant growth through a global acquisition strategy.

Danske Bank was already the Largest financial services provider in Denmark when, in 2004, the group acquired two Ireland-based entities. National Irish Bank and Northern Bank, for a total of around US $1.8 bn. In 2007 the company also acquired Sampo, a Finnish insurer, for just over US $5 bn.

Mr Mørch believes that an organisation experiencing "this level of growth" will "have great need of talent". Not surprisingly, many of the HR strategies and practices at Danske Bank today focus on talent management. Mr Mørch adds that this is, in fact "one of the most important ways we in HR can help the line managers—by helping to recruit, identify, develop and retain good people throughout the group".

A Focus on Measurement

At Danske Bank, measurement is everything. "We are fact-based in our HR approach," says Mr Mørch. "Look at any process here, and you will see that its effectiveness is being measured. We believe that all aspects of what you are doing should be based on what the numbers are telling you. Measurement is the only way you can be certain of the impact your actions are having on what you are trying to achieve."

> *Having HR strategies that march to the same beat as senior management is important when pursuing growth through global acquisition.*

Now look closely at any of a handful of HR processes, says Mr Mørch, "and you will see how we measure our effectiveness". For example, in the area of recruitment efforts, "we measure the number of applicants". But the measurement doesn't stop there. For example, three months after an applicant becomes an employee, "we check with them whether or not the job and the training we promised them is the same as what they were given; what they're experiencing," he says. Then a year into employment, "we ask them still more about their job and their relationship with their co-workers and managers".

Essentially, according to Mr Mørch, rigorous measurement of HR's effectiveness creates a cycle of continuous improvement. He believes that a similar measurement can be seen in all phases of HR at Danske Bank, from recruitment to development and retention.

The US Navy: Sharing Knowledge Electronically

When a business executive's preparation for a position is insufficient, it may cost the company in terms of revenue or profit. But when the training of an officer or sailor in the US Navy is lacking, the stakes can be significantly higher. As such, the US Navy takes its leadership development and training perhaps more seriously than most other organisations.

Ken Decker and Tony Martin are both retired chief petty officers and now full-time independent contractors. They are key members of a team whose focus within the Navy's training and development frameworks is to assess and continuously improve the effectiveness of the organisation's online knowledge management system.

Naval Knowledge: Online

According to Mr. Martin, life in the Navy is a continuous learning process. No matter how effective or thorough the formal training maybe, "there's always more a sailor needs to know". The Navy works best when more experienced sailors and officers can pass along knowledge to where it is needed. "Informal learning and knowledge sharing is vital," says Mr. Martin. This could be fundamental or technical information such as how to execute a critical task. Or, he says, it could be something as basic as "how many pairs of socks or toothbrushes to pack for a specific mission".

> *The Navy works best when more experienced sailors and officers can pass along knowledge to where it is needed.*

Clearly, notes Mr. Martin, sailors not only can, but also need to learn a great deal from one another. So one of the objectives of the Navy is to encourage and enable such knowledge-sharing through as many formal and informal mechanisms as possible. One of the principal ways the Navy is tackling this objective is by placing numerous knowledge-leveraging capabilities into a system known as Navy Knowledge Online or NKO.

NKO (https://wwwa.nko.navy.mil) is the focal point for a broad array of knowledge management, leadership and even fundamental human resources management tools. NKO, explains Mr Decker, allows sailors and officers to:

- ***Interact with Peers:*** Through NKO, Navy personnel can access chat rooms, message boards and related tools—all organised according to various "learning centres", which in turn branch into specific themes and subjects known as "communities of practice". For example, "there are areas organised by rating, areas that would provide peer support for, say, an apprentice gunner's mate", says Mr Decker. Using these tools, personnel are able to both share and obtain help and information. "This is the way the new generation communicates," confirms Mr Decker. "NKO merely enables the interactions."
- ***Interact with Mentors:*** As valuable as peer interaction may be, NKO also enables a number of informal and semi-formal mentor relationships. As Mr. Decker explains: "You'll see a thread on a message board where an officer or a more senior sailor is stepping in to help some young sailor gather some information—that's informal." But in other cases, "you might go to one of the communities and look for someone to mentor one of your people".
- ***Access E-Learning:*** The Navy gives sailors virtually unlimited "opportunities to prepare for advancement", says Mr. Martin. One of the principal means forward is by expanding an individual skill set through training. Here, the NKO enables access to a vast array of instruction. According to Mr. Decker, the Navy delivers "more than 6,000 courses" in its e-learning portfolio. In fact, e-learningis now a critical component of formal Navy training. E-learning tools that might, for example, teach

a sailor how to maintain a firearm or repair an electronic switch, says Mr. Decker, are "self-paced, allowing a sailor to progress as fast as he is able". As with nearly all of the Navy's e-learning modules, "there's a test at the end to assess competency, and it's all tracked and recorded".

- ***Manage Careers and Lives:*** Just as the HR functions of private companies endeavour to make life easier on employees, so too the Navy is using technology to try to improve enlisted life for sailors, officers and their families. For example, NKO "enables interaction with families via instant messaging", says Mr. Decker. But in addition. Navy personnel can also use NKO to gain access to tools that help them to manage their bank accounts, benefits, leave statuses, ratings, and other personal and career issues.

Coming Soon (to a battleship near you)

Although every sailor and officer in the US Navy knows and relies on NKO, granting access on anything akin to a 24/7/365 basis remains elusive. The issue today is bandwidth. "Sailors in the sand in Iraq usually don't have access to the internet," says Mr. Decker. "And a lot of ships can only get access to a limited functionality version—that's 'NKO at Sea'."

Mr. Decker adds: "In addition to making sure buttons click and the right information is getting to the right people, a big part of our assignment is looking for more ways to get more access to more people more often."

Office Depot: Finding the Right People

Unsurprisingly, Office Depot needs talent as the company is expanding aggressively in the US and globally. Today, the retailer operates approximately 1,200 retail stores in North America. But by the end of 2007, Office Depot hopes to have opened 100 more locations, with another 125-150 stores in place by the end of 2008.

In addition, Office Depot has an aggressive plan for store renovations. Over the next two to three years, the company intends to implement its new "M2" format, a retail concept intended to enhance the customer experience, at most locations. With all that is happening, JoAnne Moeller, vice-president of human resources, compensation, benefits and HR-Information managementis confident that for the right people Office Depot has a variety of great opportunities.

The Culture of Collaboration

So how does the company define "right"? Ms Moeller believes that it is important to understand certain key elements of the culture at Office Depot.

First and foremost, she says, "Office Depot is very much a culture of shared responsibility and collaboration". Getting things done requires "a lot of co-operation and shared ownership of projects. And that means finding people who not only understand how to get things done but who also understand the importance of working with others."

"We're only a 20-year-old company in an aggressive growth mode. If you come here, you're going to help us build the process."

No matter the source of the potential employee, and no matter that employee's paper qualifications, "they can expect to be interviewed extensively, much more than they're likely used to", says Ms. Moeller. "On average, there will be at least 8 to 10 interviews at certain levels. This is very much a culture where there is collective ownership of the hiring process."

Office Depot needs talent, "but that doesn't mean we're going to settle for just anyone", she adds. "In some companies, an individual is hired to become a member of an existing process. We're only a 20-year-old company in an aggressive growth mode. If you come here, you're going to help us build the processes."

According to Ms Moeller, the rigorous nature of the interviewing process becomes critical for at least two reasons.

First, "it weeds out anyone who wouldn't fit into our team-oriented and collaborative culture—and that's important because it's a very close-knit company". Second, says Ms Moeller, the cost of making a hiring mistake is too high. In her experience, the numerous perspectives gained from a process featuring multiple interviewers are highly effective in identifying issues before they become problems for the company. "If we can identify someone who might lead us down a wrong path, someone who's not fitting in, that's a lot of damage that can be avoided."

The Role of Technology

In line with its aggressive growth. Office Depot is also in the midst of revamping its underlying HR technology. "We believe we can use technology to be more efficient in HR and to do more with less," says Ms Moeller. "[Technology] can help us automate the mundane aspects of the work so we can focus more attention on the strategy."

A recently deployed and now more effective HR software and technology platform is helping the company in at least two ways. First, the new systems are helping Office Depot to "gather, evaluate and manage our HR data", says Ms Moeller. "It's helping us ensure that our performance management is more organised and more effective. It's giving us better quality and better control of our HR processes. That's particularly important in a large and fast-growing global organisation—to be able to keep track of your people wherever they might be." The value here, she adds, is "just tremendous".

Second, the new systems are helping the company to provide better HR support to its employees. "We're paying a lot more attention these days to the work-life balance," notes Ms Moeller. And one of the ways the company can give its associates more flexibility, she explains, "is by delivering more services online". With the new systems, "our associates can get the information they need, make changes such as adjusting payroll deductions or updating an address, from anywhere at any time".

Aditya Birla Group: Dealing with Rapid Growth

Dr. Santrupt Misra is the global head of HR and IT for India-based Aditya Birla Group (ABG). A conglomerate with leadership positions in a broad range of endeavours from aluminium and cement to telecoms and insurance, ABG faces many challenges in HR management. Nonetheless, says Dr. Misra, "we believe our practices are proving highly effective".

Where's the Talent?

The most visible challenge for Dr. Misra, by now a familiar refrain within this report, is "how do we attract, develop and retain our talent?" This challenge, as Dr. Misra sees it, is multi-faceted.

For example, one piece of the puzzle is figuring out "how to accelerate leadership development", he says. The company is currently experiencing double-digit growth both in India and globally, creating enormous pressure to move executives "up" in the organisation. Basically, says Dr. Misra, "new investments are proceeding almost faster than we can grow our talent".

Another related challenge is the increasingly far-flung nature of ABG's operations. As Dr. Misra explains, "not only is there great demand for leaders and talent, we need to develop managers who are capable of managing in a context of fast-changing economies and markets, and multiple cultures".

> *"In India, with the fast growth in the domestic economy, companies are always competing for the best managers—there"s a real talent shortage."*

Next up are the particular challenges of attracting and retaining talent in a high-growth emerging market. "In India," he explains, "with the fast growth in the domestic economy, companies are always competing for the best managers—there is a real talent shortage."

Finally, the critical challenge is finding a way to address all of the above issues within the context of a single set of HR policies and practices. "We are a conglomerate," he explains. "So from a technology and a strategy perspective, we have to figure out how to put in global HR processes that provide the value of a generic approach but still allow variation in the individual businesses and markets where needed."

The Solution Set

Addressing all of the above requires a comprehensive set of solutions. First of all, the company attempts to accelerate the career development of high-potential personnel, "One thing you will see here most visibly," says Dr. Misra, "is that we see to it that the empowerment levels are pushed very far down the line." In other words, "very early in a career here, you'll see people being given larger responsibilities and significant opportunities to develop competencies".

But Dr. Misra believes that, particularly in a competitive talent marketplace, there is no one size fits all solution. "You must develop people. You must show them where they fit in to the organisation. You must compensate them fairly, but, more importantly, you need to show them where they can go in the business. You need to give them training and you need to provide them with opportunities. They need to feel valued by the business."

Explosive growth meant that the company rapidly evolved beyond the capabilities of its legacy HR systems.

The Solution Set

The company also fosters development and retention by encouraging innovation. Dr. Misra says "there are certain people with great ideas and who thrive on greater responsibility". So to tap into this talent the company runs an internal programme known as adventure. The way it works, says Dr. Misra, "is that if you have a workable business idea, we tell you to come forward and develop a business plan". The best of these plans "receive the support of the company". The authors of such plans "are given leave with pay to develop their ideas to the fullest. It's a source of some great business ideas and it is very valuable for developing our people."

The group has also organised what it refers to as an assessment centre. Here, chosen high-potential executives are given opportunities for cross-cultural training with various external companies. "We run consortium programmes with six or so other companies," explains Dr Misra, trading personnel on short-to medium-term assignments. Within this framework, "we assess the participants and we can track their performance with their peers from these othercompanies".

New HR Systems

Explosive growth, says Dr. Misra, meant that the company rapidly evolved beyond the capabilities of its legacy HR systems. As such, in early 2006, the company deployed the first modules of a new and comprehensive enterprise HR package. The new technology, he insists, "will cut costs and improve quality and visibility almost immeasurably".

One of the biggest sets of benefits anticipated by Dr. Misra is standardisation. "This is a fast-growing organisation and it is diverse." But with a standardised HR platform, "when someone moves from one business to another, they don't have to learn new systems and processes". Similarly, he explains, "the rotation and tracking of people is much, much simpler".

Dr. Misra also appreciates the ability to have all information on his workforce available for data mining. "Say we need to find someone who's worked on a greenfield project outside of India, or who speaks Mandarin or Spanish and is a black belt in SixSigma," says Dr Misra. All in all, says Dr Misra, "the new technology is greatly improving our effectiveness and the quality of our decision-making".

Conclusion

Organisations across the private and public sectors, and in loca-tions ranging from North America and Western Europe to the emerging markets, are recognising that there is enormous—and often untapped—strategic value in HR. As is the case with other staff functions, organisations benefit when HR forms a collaborative partnership with business units. And some of the highest returns result when HRand business units collaborate in areas such as work-force assessment, recruitment, retention, training and development.

Integrated, scalable HR applications and processes can promote a consistent culture, plan and strategy without compromising Local nuance and effectiveness. These systems can help organisations to engage employees directly and make them responsible for their actions, which can have a direct impact on the success of the organisation. Moreover, they can do so without overburdening HR staff.

CHAPTER

4

The Tipping Point for Talent Management

*—Lt. K. Venkatarao**

In Malcolm Gladwell's book, an innovation or change can suddenly appear through small, almost incremental steps, none of which by itself is especially noteworthy. But the combination of these seemingly minor events can cause organizations to be shaken, countries to be impacted and people to break out of established behavioural patterns. What could not be accomplished in one grand wave of the baton is, in fact, being accomplished by different pieces of the puzzle coming together at just the right time.

We are in the midst of such a sea change in the field of talent management. This new approach to managing companies and people has not yet become a clearly articulated science. There is still too much to understand and learn about the shifts occurring before us. But there is an emerging set of practices—especially as evidenced by industry-leading companies—that are moving talent management to its tipping point.

*Sr. Lecturer in Commerce, Govt. College (A), Rajahmundry, A.P.

The Changing Business Context

The current economic environment sets the foundation for the reason that talent management practices have arisen in the first place. Bossidy and Charan (2004) have identified five different economic stages that have existed during the past century. Others have talked more generally about the movement from agrarian to industrial to the knowledge economy. Pink (2005) describes the next step as moving from the knowledge age to the conceptual age, while Friedman (2005) discusses many of these same shifts in terms of 'Globalization 3.0'. While neither of these terms has resonated with wider audiences, there is no doubt that we are entering a post-knowledge worker economic stage-whatever it may be called.

The management models and systems from past stages tend to be the first ones applied in new stages. These, after all, have been what executives know, understand and have experienced. Past success becomes a blinder for future achievements, because it is natural to think that what worked once, should work again. It takes years and even decades for new models and practices to emerge.

Most of our current management practices are mired in the past and based on a set of assumptions that no longer exist. The sidebar opposite highlights many of these differences. Consider this list and assess your own company's position.

Many companies are at a spot along this continuum with one foot in the past and another in the future. Some of these factors may not be as important as others, but it is becoming increasingly clear that old practices will not be effective in a future that requires innovation, fast responses, horizontal relationships, high engagement levels and optimum performance from assets that are not "owned" by the company. Perhaps this is why in this transition period, 75 per cent of change managements fail, less than 10 per cent of companies do a good job of implementing their own strategy, and the vast majority of mergers and acquisitions fail to meet their objectives. New mindsets and practices are needed for new times.

Globalization

"Today, the most profound thing is that a 14 year old in Romania or Bangalore or Vietnam has all the information, all the tools, all the software easily available to apply knowledge however they want."

Perhaps the biggest contributor to the talent management tipping point is the new global marketplace. More than any single factor it has caused us to consider how fast change can take place, and how firmly held beliefs are wavering or are no longer valid. The world is a very different place than it was even at the start of the century, barely six years ago. Consider the following examples:

- Billions of people are new entrants into the world economy and entire nations have skipped stages of economic growth to get there faster than anyone could have anticipated.
- The talented minds of foreign born nationals are returning to their home country rather than contributing to the human capital of Western Europe and the United States.
- China is revamping its educational system to focus less on rote memorization and more on creativity and innovation.
- Ireland is the world's largest exporter of software.
- The business incentives and infrastructure offered by many 'developing countries' is equal to or better than the environment in the so-called 'richer nations'.
- Three countries that excel in new scientific and technical talent are India, China and Russia.

- Talent pools, just like markets, exist all over the world and are no longer the exclusive province of Western countries.
- Microsoft's R&D center in Beijing is the best performing software research unit in the corporation.
- Outsourcing and offshoring are not just about cheaper wages and low cost services, but also about access to talent.

The companies that will win in this post-knowledge economy may not be those that were the most successful in past stages.

"Intel goes where the IQ is" Tom Friedman The World is Flat.

Integrated Talent Management Wheel

Talent is now a global game. It requires a much broader horizon than just a specific company, city, region or country. And it requires a much broader vision even within a company. The Talent Wheel highlights the key talent functions that need to be co-ordinated and integrated within organizations.

Workforce planning looks at the supply and demand for talent over a two-year or longer period of time for key jobs within the enterprise. Key issues are retirements, planned and unplanned attrition, varying staffing options, competencies for superior performers and bench strength for key talent.

Talent acquisition is the ability of a company to attract and hire key talent. This is one of the two most pressing needs according to Accenture's 2005 survey of global executives. Key issues are compelling employment brand and value propositions, referral recruiting, and keeping a gold standard for new talent entering the organization.

Talent engagement represents the extent to which the workforce identifies with the company, is committed to it and provides discretionary effort so that it can be successful. Engagement is a key leading indicator for high performance workplaces, improved employee productivity and subsequent turnover. Keep engagement surveys relatively short and ensure that data are acted upon by employees and managers.

Talent development used to be synonymous with training, but no longer. Research shows that 70 per cent of what we need to know to do our job, we learn on the job. Informal learning is more powerful than formal learning through such activities as stretch assignments, cross-functional teams, international assignments and flexible job design.

Talent deployment can be summarized as the right people are doing the right job at the right time. Top talent is assigned to the most vital projects or roles. Alignment is a key aspect of talent deployment, and it is most often achieved through performance management systems and competency databases matching project needs to employee capabilities.

The ability to lead talent is also key. Great managers are like chess players who understand that different pieces (employees) have unique strengths (Buckingham, 2004), and these managers work hard to put employees in positions where they can shine. Great managers also understand that their value to the organization is through the contributions of others, and it is their responsibility to develop, guide and enhance the performance of the people that report to them.

Talent retention is the number one issue on the minds of global executives according to the Accenture study (2005). Many CEOs doubt their company's ability to retain top talent. Too little and too much turnover can damage a business. It is interesting to observe that when managers of departing employees are asked why a person left, money is the overwhelming answer. When the employees themselves are asked, money doesn't even make the top five.

These talent functions must work together and be part of a seamless system. Being excellent in one or two areas is a start, but the whole system must be working effectively. It does little good, for example, for a company to attract and hire great talent but then have few challenging development opportunities. Similarly, for CEOs to focus compulsively on retention misses the point that retention probably wouldn't be a problem if talent engagement, development and deployment functions were smoothly operating.

These talent functions are too important to be left to separate departments, silos or champions. The essence of a company's ability to compete rests with the optimization and integration of these functions—it is the network, not the nodes that provide the value.

The Tipping Point

Talent management is ready to be tipped. First, there is the growing amount of empirical evidence that shows a clear relationship between excellent talent practices and improved shareholder returns. Among the providers of this research are McKinsey, Gallup, Collins, Bassi, Watson & Wyatt, Decker and Huselid, and the Fortune Best Places to Work surveys.

Second, there are the best practices from companies that truly believe that talent is the essence of their success. Among these companies are GE, Dell, P&G, HSBC, FedEx, Starbucks, Microsoft and Capital One, to name just a few.

Third, there is the growing realization that talent issues are board level issues. More investment analysts and company directors are demanding to know about engagement levels, segmented turnover data, and the types of developmental opportunities for top talent. CEOs are starting to spend 30 per cent or more of their time on talent issues, and are being held accountable for the strength of their talent pools. For instance, all companies registered in Denmark will be required to include in their annual reports information about customers, processes and human capital. A minimum of five measures for each is required and comparisons with the previous two years must be shown. Information for investors about intellectual capital both current and future should occupy at least one-third of the report.

The confluence of both internal and external factors is causing a new science of talent management to emerge and tip. This is very different from traditional human resources concerns. While HR is more concerned with consistency, compliance and treating everyone in the same fashion, talent management recognizes that different people make different contributions to the enterprise, and that top talent is the key to competitive differentiation. The seamless and integrated functioning of the talent management wheel is what will drive companies into a leadership position in the new, post-knowledge economy.

CHAPTER

5

Talent Management

How to Retain Top Talent without Derailing the Organization when Fast Tracking

*—Mr. Roopesh Kumar Misra**

Most people would not choose to build a house on a weak foundation. Why then do leaders risk the company's future on an untested, inexperienced employee?

To keep them motivated?

To ensure they stay with the company?

But at what cost—to the employee, the employees who work for them and the company.

Yes, if you want to retain your top employees, you must...

1. Give them a reason to stay
2. Find a way to motivate them
3. Reward them.

But, if you reward too much, too fast—it can be dangerous for your entire organization.

*Mr. Misra is a Project Manager and Research Scholar working at Mumbai.

In order for companies to retain top talent and stay competitive in today's market they are engaging in fast tracking. This means they are moving selected employees quickly to or through managerial levels in an organization.

5 Reasons Why Fast Tracking is a Dangerous Strategy for Increasing Employee Retention.

1. Skills can be learned quickly; experience takes time. In order to be an effective leader, your managers need to gain experience in:

- Correctly identifying and solving problems
- Framing and making good decisions
- Dealing with the myriad of people-related issues that confront every manager in every organization
- Organization course correction
- Role-based leadership.

2. Many times, when your organization engages in fast tracking, a new manager will set a new initiative in motion and then leave the position before the impact of the initiative is realized. They are missing the day-to-day experience of interpersonal behaviours and interactions that come with any transition—the intangible. It's these subtleties that are often missed. And it's these subtleties and the way you handle them that hones a good leader.

3. Each managerial level brings new challenges and requires different skills and behaviours. Moving too quickly through an organization runs the risk of missing critical experiential learning. Experience is accretive and it is difficult to learn vicariously. What you learn today you use as a framework for how you behave and react tomorrow. Short changing this learning cycle can result in a leader derailing later.

4. When leaders derail because a company engaged in fast tracking in order to retain top talent, it creates a

disastrous domino effect for the organization as a whole. We all know that the number one reason people leave a company is because of their immediate supervisor. We also know that poor decisions and poor problem solving skills can result in service and profitability deterioration for a company.

5. Fast tracking creates a winner/loser environment within the company. Unless you want to build a highly-competitive, stressful environment and internal culture that makes your employees hate Mondays because it is the start of a work week, creating winners and losers is not a good long-term strategy.

Why Companies Engage in Fast Tracking Even Though It's Dangerous to the Health of their Organization.

Companies need to grow talent internally and insure smooth management transitions. And the reality is that some industries are disproportionally affected by talent shortages (such as health care) and may have no other choice than to promote an employee who is truly not ready to handle the position.

(This is a common practice for technical and clinical staff promoted to management).

So what should you do?

7. Tips for Retaining Top Talent Without Hurting Your New Manager, Employees and the Company

1. Develop a succession plan for your company. This means get committed to a process or structure of internal management and talent development.
2. Identify individuals within the organization who have the potential to move into leadership positions. You should be identifying multiple candidates for each position. Don't be afraid to take some risks in candidate identification. Not all high potential candidates initially present an outgoing and aggressive demeanor (and

remember these qualities do not necessarily ensure a good manager.)

3. Provide the identified individuals with opportunities to take on additional projects to demonstrate their skills as well as their ability to learn and grow. The projects should create the opportunity for the candidates to "live" with the consequences and take responsibility for their actions and decisions.
4. Provide new managers with an internal mentor and an external coach to insure support during the transition process. This support should be for at least six months to one year. This process is referred to as: "transition integration".
5. Give all new managers a personality and job performance assessment. This is a valuable tool in identifying emerging leader attributes and potential risk areas. Now you will be able to enable early intervention and prevention and give the most effective support to the new manager. This is better than the "sink or swim" approach to learning that new managers are often thrown into.
6. Provide all candidates with self-assessment tools and learning opportunities. Do this both within the organization in the form of added responsibilities and through outside learning opportunities such as conferences and executive education programmes, professional memberships.
7. Monitor your new manager's progress (through the supervisor and mentoring and coaching support) and review your succession plan each year. Evaluate the success of the current programme and the individuals in the programme. Improve where necessary and identify and support new leadership candidates.

Be aware that some candidates simply may not be interested in this, more protracted and performance based approach. They may feel threatened or choose to leave. That's OK too. The risk of promoting too quickly and the derailment that could occur is not worth the harm an unprepared manager can bring to the organization.

Talent is to be developed, not anointed.

CHAPTER

6

Talent Management Challenges

*—Dr. Haribandi Srinivas Rao**

Talented person is an individual with bright abilities. A person who has multi-skills and is self-motivated, has excellent knowledge and high general competencies (communicating, IQ, leadership).

Talented Specialist = Productivity + Competency + Easy Learning

It is the process of developing and integrating new workers, developing and retaining current workers, and attracting highly skilled workers, to work for a company. The 'war for talent' has focused on acquiring and assimilating ' the best'. Human resources play a significant role in reaching organization effectiveness and performance ((Husclid, 1995). Talent has become the key differentiator for human capital management and for leveraging competitive advantage (Bhatnagar, 2004). A talent management strategy generally covers an Organization's approach towards recruitments and

*Dr. Haribandi Srinivas Rao, Sr. Lect. in Commerce, Badruka College of Commerce, Kachiguda, Hyderabad-27, A.P.

retention assessment and evaluation, compensation and benefits, performance management, learning, development and succession planning Technological advances and global competition are the main drivers of changes in employment patterns leading to intense competition between employers to attract and retain talented workers.

According to "Global Talent Management Survey of HR Professionals", the areas of priority where knowledge technology is most needed are:

- Succession planning;
- Career and development planning;
- Talent profiles;
- Recruitment, hiring, applicant tracking;
- Workforce measurement;
- Leadership development.

Dr. Haribandi Srinivas Rao, Sr. Lect. in Commerce, Badruka College of Commerce, Kachiguda, Hyd-27, A.P.

Objectives of the Study

The Present study has been undertaken with the following objectives:

1. to trace the roots of talent development;
2. to highlight the need and importance of talent mgt. in Indian corporate sector;
3. to identify the areas of talent development in Indian corporate sector;
4. to present the finds of the study in the form of conclusion to strengthen the field of talent management.

Methodology

The Primary aim of this paper is to investigate the areas of talent development in Indian companies. The data collected includes, primary data collected through interview method and secondary data collected from previous records, reference books and internet.

Why Talent Management is the Need of the Hour?

After years of paying lip service to the notion—"our workforce is our greatest asset", organizations are now beginning to take action on the same. It is high time that firms plan and execute talent management for requisite results to survive in this competitive age. The soaring costs and risks associated with human resources; and the direct dependence of customers and brand equity on the employee talent pool, requires firms to effectively attract, motivate and nurture talent. The cost benefit analysis of talent cum competencies development is essential at every level by the head of the HR department. Let us take a look at the reasons that make talent management a vital cog in the growth wheel of organization.

- ***Cost Constrains:*** It is a known fact nowadays that HR management is becoming a highly capital—intensive function of an organization. Right from the direct costs related to recruitment, training, remuneration and developmental efforts, to the indirect costs associated with attrition and poor planning, manpower administration require a careful planning and execution at every step. With the demand for talent going up disproportionately in relation to its supply, the cost of attracting, developing and retaining this talent has emerged as an area of serious concern for the HR managers. Once, such as investment is made by an organization on the personnel, it is inevitable to guard it so as to reap the returns.
- ***Unavoidable Perils:*** Talent management efforts have always been a big gamble for the firms. Even if utmost planning and caution is exercised, managers cannot completely write-off the chances of failure resulting from new staff not performing as expected. Besides, there is

always a lurking danger that the talent pool may leave the organization despite all the measures being taken to ensure its sustenance in the long-run. Such risks can be decreased but never completely mitigated.

- ***Customer Relationships:*** Employees bind the customers to the organizations as a glue, and if that relationship is broken as a result of key talent leaving the organization, the capacity of the firm to provide sustainable service to its clients is severely compromised. This has the potential to compromise future business and customer base.
- ***Survival and Growth:*** With increasing globalization and proliferation of competitors, it is the responsibility of the organizations to make, built and nourish their talent pool that decides their survival in the long-run. Besides, the role of talented employees in giving a sustainable competitive advantage is obvious and efforts to effectively manage this talent become a driving wheel for the growth and development of organizations.

In the light of the above reasons, it is obligatory for organizations to invest their time, energy and resources to improve workforce productivity. As firms seek new ways of dealing with current policy changes, 'talent management' has become a vital element in establishing a Human Capital Management (HCM) environment.

Identification of Talent

The employees are assessed through competency framework. The methodology used for the assessment and development of manpower is through the e-map cycle. This is the foundation for an outstanding talent management programme. Identification of talent is directly related to higher motivation and performance of an employee. Set the realistic target for an individual that must be in line with the organizational goals. Employees need a periodic feedback to check their performances. Effective performance appraisal programme is a vital part of the overall talent management system. A proper balance between evaluation of present performance and the reward system within the organization helps the employees remain motivated toward attaining personal and organizational goals.

Individual Development Planning

Managers concerned with their departments must ascertain individual short-term and long-term aspirations after analysis of jobs through e-map and performance system. The individual development is always based on self management and self development attitude of employees.

Recruiting and Retaining Talent

Talent is invisible and knowledge is visible. Talent empowerment implies competencies development.

There are two ways to procure talent, develop it from inside the organization or recruit it from inside the organization or recruit it from inside. The internal recruitment programme ensures that those candidates who have strong skills and knowledge are self-motivated and emotionally stable, actually know how to make things happen in the organization and have potential abilities to fulfil the demands of customers and also to align with the company's goals. Such candidates may be promoted through various ways in the organization. Candidates who are recruited from outside the organization are based on their academic records and certain predetermined competencies through a proper selection procedure.

Areas of Improvement for Retaining Talent

Focusing on talent retention programme is every businesses' top priority. Every employee discusses his/her area of improvement with his/her boss. There are various learning activities which involves both employees and organization. Retention of employees must start with the right hiring process of employees, identifying potential candidates early and focusing on different issues to retain talent, such as:

- Encourage the quality relationship with boss.
- Involve them in decision-making process.
- Build a learning culture where creativity, new skills and self development is encouraged.
- Manage balance between work and home life.
- Provide opportunities for growth and advancement for existing employees.
- Provide guidance, performance counseling and employee assistance programmes.
- Provide challenging task for demonstrating their competency.
- Expanding training and development practices.
- Provide motivation, co-operation, external rewards and trust to retain the employees.
- Introducing employee engagement and branding programme.
- Company's clear vision and objectives help employees to align their own personal objectives.
- Introduce new technologies to handle day-to-day operations.

Stress Management Programmes

Stress is the one factor that constantly looms large over modern lifestyles. It can wrap its iron first around you and slowly yet steadily take over entire life if you don't deal with it at the right time.

Stress is a condition or feeling experienced when a person perceives that demands exceed the personal and social resources he/she is able to mobilize "Stress is an inseparable part of human existence and we need a minimum amount of stress to work affectively. However, we need to differentiate normal stress from abnormal stress".

Increased stress can cause a large number of health related problems affecting the psychological, biological, physical and social functioning of a person. Some ways of identifying abnormal stress levels is by recognizing the behavioural and emotional symptoms associated with it. The behavioural symptoms include substance dependence, sleep problems, increased smoking, restlessness, eating problems, irritation, accident prone, low productivity and bad time management. The emotional symptoms include anxiety, guilt, embarrassment, depression, jealousy, feel like dying, crying frequently, feeling moody, emptiness and aggression. It can be associated with physical symptoms like pounding of heart, sweating, shaking of hands, giddiness and choking sensation.

The common complication of stress include digestion problems, blood pressure, heart problems, tiredness, allergies, low immunity, decreased sexual activity and psychiatric disorders like substance abuse, depression, anxiety disorders and poor interpersonal relationships.

"If normal stress management techniques like positive thinking, identifying the source of stress, setting goals and acting on it, prioritizing etc. do not work for you and stress is taking over a larger part of your life then seeking professional intervention is extremely important", the growing problems related with stress and the lack of proper emotional support systems in modern society has resulted in the need for mental and emotional health care facilities. Further, HR relived from stress contributes to organizational productivity quality of work life and burnout issues. Hence, there is a linear relationship between talent development and productivity improvement.

Explore Ways and Means for Involving the CEO

Talent management initiatives cannot make much headway without the support and involvement of the top management, in general, and CEO, in particular, Active support and involvement of the CEOs can manifest itself by way of sharing the virtues of talent with the employees. Towards this end, CEOs may convene a social meeting of sorts to discuss about talent specific issues, conduct leadership conclaves and high-power programmes. For example, iconic CEO, Jack Welch of GE, spends the better part of his time on talent centric matters. He understands that talent is the cornerstone of any business and attunes himself to the aspirations and requirements of the critical talent. It behooves HR departments to look for ways to involve CEOs in the talent management initiatives.

Conclusion

Talent management is here to stay for a long haul and it may change the way HR departments function. Increasingly, technologies are getting more evolved and may further bolster the talent management in a more ways than one. Clearly, the inevitability of talent management is not lost on management and employees. For the HR professionals, talent management initiatives could be a magic wand that will help them to hone their skills and raise their profile to find their pride of place on the board and increase their elbow room with top management. So what is stopping HR professionals? Come on guys! Jump on to the "Talent Management Bandwagon" and the "World is your Oyster".

REFERENCES

1. HRM Review, the ICFAI University Press, Feb, 2010 by NR Aravamudhan, Assistant Professor, M.I.T., Tamil Nadu.
2. HRM Review, the ICFAI University Press, Aug, 2010 by Garima Bardia, Research Scholar, University of Rajasthan, Jaipur.
3. HRM Review, the ICFAI University Press, Nov, 2010 by Geeta Rana and Dr. Pooja Garg, LIT, Roorkee, Uttarakhand.
4. Times of India, 20th November, 2010.

CHAPTER

7

Managing Talent after 2020 in Global Scenario

***Judhisthir Pradhan**

****Prof. (Dr.) R.N. Misra**

'When land was the productive, nations battled over it. The same is happing now for talented people".

Stan Device & Christopher Meyer, future Wealth

Introduction

Talent may be understood as an attribute of high and artistic ability with special aptitude. Longman's Active Study Dictionary defines "Talent" as *"A Special internal Quality"*. Talent may be considered a man who creates value in an organization needs to succeed. Management can be coined as "The optimum utilization of scared resource". When we use the word "Talent management" it definitely indicates towards a corporation or towards any organization. "Talent Management could be understood as "Nurturing and

*Mr. Pradhan, Lecturer in Marketing and Finance, College of Advance Computing, Berhampur.

**Prof. (Dr.) Misra, HOD, Human Resource Studies, PGCMS, SMIT, Berhampur.

developing those people identified as having ability and potential", and it should form part of recruitment and retention strategy. Last two and half and decades is witness of the massive globalization. Today's global marketplace is swapping the industrialization of the global workforce. To remain a leader in the face of global competition, organizations must carefully leverage the best talent available at the lowest possible cost. This entitles a thoughtful approach to talent management after 2020. In a recent survey of more than 1000 clients, management consultant firm PI world wide discovered 52 per cent of companies identified "Leadership development" as their top employee development for outpacing "teamwork" mentioned by 28 per cent. Given to-day's dynamic global hypercompetitive marketplace and the accompanying scarcity of talent, it is clear companies are increasingly recognizing the need to identify, develop and retain high caliber leaders.

Scope and Objective of the Paper

- ***Need of Qualitative Analysis of Talent***

In the present scenario of the globalization, qualitative analysis of talent is highly essential. As there are a lot of qualified and certificate holders now a days. The organizations now have a lot of alternatives for recruiting their workforce. Corporations in the present time expect something different and something wonder from their personnel. Due to globalization in education and technology a lot of talent from abroad is now flowing into country to country. Hence, there are very less chance of not getting a right person for the right job. So now a days it is globally believed that quality and quickness is key scale for measurement of skill.

- ***Technological Advancement***

Day by day we are growing in terms of technology. A technically advanced nation and organization as well, can grow like anything. It is not only the engineers who must be aware of new technology but also the managers must have required knowledge about the technology. A correct technology definitely gives good mileage to any short of business. Correct technology can make a big difference in productivity and quality management.

- ***Market Requirement and Competition***

Four P's *i.e.* price, product, place and promotion what we call marketing mix plays very vital role to convert the investment into return. Better marketing strategy and responding to the customers as per their need boosts to go ahead and achieve the goal. The present market demands energetic, dynamic, elegant, confident, good looking and smart personnel to give better mileage to the business. Similarly competition of the present time definitely adds a new dimension to the marketing strategy. The throat cut competition emphases on the selection of the best person for the assignment. No one loves to loose the market place and market share.

- ***Nature of Business***

As per the business *i.e.* the kind of the business also have similar impact on the recruitment and training of the personnel. As per the kind of the business it's employees should be selected and trained.

- ***Business Culture and Performance***

Business culture is an important factor that motivates the employee to work up to their at best level. A real talented person always love to work hard and love to the best output of the inputs given to him. But at the same time he cannot compromise with dissatisfied scrounging, as talent always has demand, one loves to quit the organization. The relationship between the employees, the interpersonal and intrapersonal relationships must be maintained in the organization. There should be mutual understanding and respect. The performance is the only measure of any talent. The level of performance and the perfection of the performance helps to point out talent and boost them.

- ***Development of Employee***

Every employee having three basic requirements which must be satisfied by the organization. They are: (*i*) Economical requirements; (*ii*) Physical and Psychological requirements; and (*iii*) updation of technological requirement. Talent management is having the responsibility to provide the above to the required persons. As per the talent the persons must get their required rights. A constant learning and development programme is required.

- ***Development of Leadership***

It indicates the development programmes for employees with high potential. As per the capability and potential every employee must get the right opportunities to prove and develop themselves.

- ***Government Guidelines and Policies***

The government of various countries are also giving many guide lines to improve the quality and potential of the employee. Every organization has to follow and obey some rules and regulations set by the government.

Importance of Talent Management

Globalization itself depicts the importance of talent management. In the global market where lot of alternatives is available for the customers, every organization desperately needs the best utilization of the talent they have. Hence, it has become a challenge for any HR personnel to recruit the best out of the bests. Some to the facts given below which advocate in favour of talent management:

- 90 per cent of organizations are experiencing recruiting difficulties.

- 85 per cent of organizations are experiencing retention problems.
- 60 per cent of employees leaving their employer reported greater promotion of development opportunities outside the company.
- 65 per cent of HR Directors said they would not re-employ their workforce.
- 85 per cent of people have leaved the managers not their jobs.
- The talent management market is expected to surpass $10 bn by 2015.
- The of recruitment of a middle manager is between 35 to 70 per cent of the annual salary (add./agency fees + HR and management time + 50 per cent effectiveness in first 3 months.).

The above facts shows the importance of talent management in the present time. Hence, failure of managing the human capital *i.e.* the talent of the organization definitely impact the immediately and directly. Followings are some of the consequences arise due to misutilization of the talent.

- Avoidable replacement cost incurred.
- Downgrade in business performance caused by increased time for external applicants to assimilate the organization culture and to provide a real return on investment.
- Development spend wasted as good qualified personnel leave.
- More management time wasted in performance management and development.

Benefits of Talent Management

Human capital is one of the most important aspect of all kinds of organization. After all it is the human being who will work and convert the paper based plans into the visible development of the organization. The role of capable workforce cannot be ignored in a successful organization. If an organization is having good and skilled workforce it may overcome any instances of difficulties. Better human resource management processes like workforce planning, skill management, recruiting and resource scheduling etc. can make big differences in the organization. Better talent management helps the organization in various ways.

- ***Organizational Benefits of Talent Management***

In order to make the strategic plans the talent management is helpful in the following ways:

- Optimizing the organization's financial investment and knowing its people and their skill.
- Improving and streamlining management's decision-making process by providing easy access to high quality information.
- Driving responsibility for skill development and career management of the employee.
- Creating a comprehensive and flexible system which will helpful for the organizational growth without occurring human resource management cost.
- Facilitating and supporting the alignment of organizational sub units and individual goals and objectives.
- Enabling the organization to strategically inventory and develop workforce skill, in order to ensure adequate supply of the skill required to meet the organization's current and future needs.
- Highlighting the strategic nature of talent management.
- Fostering improved workflow between sub-functions within HR by creating stronger linkage between them.

- ***Financial Benefits***

- Reduction in administrative efforts of approximately sixty per cent or more on the part of HR and IT staff in developing, rolling out and enforcing policies and procedures.

- Time saving of approximately 10-15 hrs per supervisor per review period.
- Time saving of approximately 3-9 hrs per employee per review period.
- Reduction in the cost of "people programmes" of approximately 20 per cent.
- Reduction in voluntary turnover of approximately 25 per cent or more.

- ***Other Benefits***

There are some other benefits too in the proper talent management. The benefit may be bundled as:

- Ensuring that decision about recruiting, selection, promotion and staffing are made with best information and maximizing the speed and effectiveness of these decisions.
- Helpful in administrating management processes.
- Helpful in increasing productivity.
- People programs give higher return.
- Streamlining the execution of the talent management process for both HR person and the managers.
- Ensuring that employee rewards are linked to the achieving of both individual and organizational objective.
- Helpful in facing the crises and difficulties.
- Helpful in competency and skill management.
- Helpful in evaluating performance.
- Helpful in career and succession planning.

Classification of Talent

Talent may be classified under the following heads.

Directly Productive Talent

The entrepreneurs, engineers, technicians, technology innovators and business creators are those persons who are included in the activities which directly effects the production of goods and services. Love to take risk and face new challenges, dare to think differently, courage of standing off bit and dream to make possible the impossible are some natures of this kind of talent.

Academic Talent

This includes the mobility of the scientists, scholars and international students. These are individual that often work or study in universities, research centers and think tanks and are devoted to the production and/or acquisition of scientific and scholarly knowledge that may be eventually in commercially valuable products and inputs.

Talent in Social and Cultural Sectors

The Society where we live and the culture which we obey is one of the important and most essential factor of our life and life style. No one can ignore that the health is a prime factor of all sorts of consideration. Everyone loves to have a good health. To maintain good health, medical and health workers and their counseling are very much essential. The talent related to the medical and health related issues are the critical social issues. Hence, mobility of doctors, nurses and other related persons directly impact the issue. Similarly the persons who are related to the culture such as poets, writers, painters, musicians, film actors, film directors, fashion designers, spiritual gurus etc also impact directly to the society.

Role of Talent Management in Management and Marketing

Talent management plays very significant role in development of the organization and the employee too. As per the managerial point of view, every manager loves to have best talent with them and utilize them the wisest way to achieve the prosperity. A talented person never loves to give chance to have a complain against him. Hence he always loves to complete the assignment in time at any cost. He never allows the work to ride him rather than loves to clutch over the assignment. A talent person may solve many critical problems by his wisdom and loves to set a new trend of his own. Once the great Bill Gates had said that, "I always assign the most difficult job to the laziest person of my organization. He finds the most easiest way of the solution for me." It emphasizes that how talent may solve critical situations. Similarly in marketing point of views, the dynamic and talented people only make the miracle. It is always said that it not only the product but the man behind the product who makes the sale. The 3C concept of marketing is totally based on the talent of the marketing executive. It is only the talent of the sales executive which convinces us to buy even a non branded product from an unknown executive. Followings are the two main functional areas where talent plays key role.

In Managerial Function

The managerial function includes planning, organizing, staffing, co-ordinating, directing, controlling and reviewing activities. Talent is one of the factors by virtue of which the above activities depend. As per Shiv Khera, the famous author of the book "You Can Win", says, "Winners don't do any different work, they do the work differently." This signifies that talent only can change the statistics. A talented manager and control the employees well and can use their potential up to the zenith level. Because he knows that when and where what will be the requirement of the employees. The perfect talented one can handle any situation in the most perfect effective way. Perfection is most essential in every field of management. Hence, in managerial function the place of the talent is at the top.

In Marketing Function

Every producer or marketer always in search of profit. Profit is the one of the major goals that every marketer or producer dreams for. Followings are some important marketing functions where talent is highly required.

- Marketing research and information management.
- Advertising and sales promotion.
- Product planning and promotion.
- Selling and physical distribution.
- Selecting, targeting and positioning of the product.
- Pricing, policy and strategy making.
- Managing and distributing the channels.

Talent Development Programme

The development programme of talent management must start from the root level. As it is not a single step action and requires huge concentration as well as effective planning. A good leader always inspires, motivates and energizes the followers. Hence, the talent development programme should be under the supervision of a good leader. Strategies must be architecture and executed to set and achieve goals, resolve conflicts and strengthen understanding and harmony. While developing the programme one must keep in mind the requirements and essential needs of the employees on which the programmes are based. There must be hierarchical approach between the successive levels of development. The development programmes again suits the organizational culture and ethics. It must work to achieve overall growth of the organization as well as the growth of the employee. The programmes must be cost effective, time bounded and fruitful. The roadmap may be designed as follows:

- Pointing out the real talent by using proper HR tools.
- Giving them proper and required training and opportunity.

- Placing them in the most appropriate work place.
- Providing performance appraisal.
- Giving them appropriate growth.

Conclusion

Every one requires the real talent for his organization. Without talented hands it is very difficulty to survive in the marketplace. Hence, finding out and implementing the real talent is definitely a big challenge. Understanding the talent, potential and skill is one part of the job. But implementing them is equally difficult and challenging too. So many factors are there which create obstacle for the implementation of the real talent. But selecting the talented person for the right purpose at the right time and engaging them in the right place for achieving the ultimate goal of the organization. After 2020 there will be huge competition between the fresher and the experienced hands. At one end there will be strong, energetic and enthusiastic hands and minds and on the other hand there will be experienced hands eagerly waiting for the new opportunities. Selection for the right candidate will be a very challenging task. Detachment, honesty, spirituality and the positive sense of responsibility may help the personnel or the recruiters to recruit the right talent and manage them in the most appropriate way.

REFERENCES

1. *Human Resource Management*: by C.B. Gupta, Sultan Chand Publication.
2. *Human Resource Management:* by Gary Dessler, Pearson Publication.
3. *A Conceptual Approach to Strategic Talent Management:* by Tapomay Dev, Indus Publishing Company.
4. *The Talent Management Book:* by D.R. Berger and L.A. Burger, Tata McGraw-Hill.

CHAPTER

8

Talent Management

—*B. Polisu, M. Com.**

Talent management refers to the skills of attracting highly skilled workers, of integrating new workers, and developing and retaining current workers to meet current and future business objectives. Talent management in this context does not refer to the management of entertainers. Companies engaging in a talent management strategy shift the responsibility of employees from the human resources department to all managers throughout the organization. The process of attracting and retaining profitable employees, as it is increasingly more competitive between firms and of strategic importance, has come to be known as "the war for talent." Talent management is also known as HCM (Human Capital Management).

The term "talent management" means different things to different organizations. To some it is about the management of high-worth individuals or "the talented" whilst to others it is about how talent is managed generally—*i.e.* on the assumption that all people have talent.

*Principal, Govt. Degree College (Men), Srikakulam-532001, Andhra Pradesh.

Evaluations

From a talent management standpoint, employee evaluations concern two major areas of measurement: *performance and potential.* Current employee performance within a specific job has always been a standard evaluation measurement tool of the profitability of an employee. However, talent management also seeks to focus on an employee's potential, meaning an employee's future performance, if given the proper development of skills and increased responsibility.

Competencies and Talent Management

This term "talent management" is usually associated with competency-based management. Talent management decisions are often driven by a set of organizational core competencies as well as position-specific competencies. The competency set may include knowledge, skills, experience, and personal traits (demonstrated through defined behaviours). Older competency models might also contain attributes that rarely predict success (*e.g.* education, tenure, and diversity factors that are illegal to consider in relation to job performance in many countries, and unethical within organizations). New techniques involve creating a Competency architecture for the organization that includes a Competency dictionary to hold the competencies in order to build job descriptions.

Talent Market Place

A talent market place is an employee training and development strategy that is set in place within an organization. It is found to be most beneficial for companies where the most productive employees can pick and choose the projects and assignments that are most ideal for the specific employee. An ideal setting is where productivity is employee centric and tasks are described as "judgment-based work," for example, in a law firm. The point of activating a talent marketplace within a department is to harness and link individuals' particular skills (project management or extensive knowledge in a particular field) with the task at hand. Examples of companies that implement the talent marketplace strategy are American Express and IBM.

Current Application of Talent Management

In current economic conditions, many companies have felt the need to cut expenses. This should be the ideal environment to execute a talent management system as a means of optimizing the performance of each employee and the organization. However, within many companies the concept of human capital management has just begun to develop. "In fact, only 5 per cent of organizations say they have a clear talent management strategy and operational programmes in place today."

Talent Review

To develop a clear talent management strategy and to increase awareness of available talent and successors, all organizations should conduct regular Talent Review meetings to be prepared for a variety of business changes, such as mergers, company growth, or a decrease in talent needs. In the same way that all companies have regular meetings and reports regarding their financial status and budgetary needs, the Talent Review meeting is designed to review the current talent status and future successor needs in the organization.

The Talent Review meeting is an important part of the overall talent management process; it is designed to review the performance and career potential of employees, to discuss possible vacancy risks of current employees, to identify successors and top talent in the organization, and to create development action plans to prepare employees for future roles in the organization. "This is what talent management is all about — gathering information about talent, analyzing their career interests and organizational business needs, identifying top talent and successes, and developing these individuals to reduce the risk of losing the best people and experiencing extensive leadership gaps when turnover occurs."

Talent Drives Performance

We all know that teams with the best people perform at a higher level. Leading organizations know that exceptional business performance is driven by superior talent. People are the difference. Talent management is the strategy.

Analyst research has proven that organizations using Talent Management strategies and solutions exhibit higher performance than their direct competitors and the market in general. From Fortune 100 global enterprise recruiting and performance management to small and medium business e-Recruiting, leading companies invest in talent management to select the best person for each job because they know success is powered by the total talent quality of their workforce.

The Talent Age

In 1997, a McKinsey study coined the term: war for talent. Now in the new millennium, we find ourselves in the talent age. During the agricultural age, the economy was based on land, a truly physical and very tangible asset. The industrial age followed with a manufacturing-driven economy. Higher business performance was derived through the most effective use of factories and distribution networks.

The knowledge age moved the basis of economic value to information assets through integrated communications and computer technology. Now the competitive battlefront is for the best people because they are the true creators of value.

- The New HR Mission and Talent Management Processes.
- Many challenging workforce issues confront HR, including:
- Heightened competition for skilled workers.

- Impending retirement of the baby boomers.
- Low levels of employee engagement.
- Acknowledgement of the high cost of turnover.
- Arduous demands of managing global workforces.
- Importance of succession planning.
- Off shoring and outsourcing trends.

This requires new thinking and a new mission to achieve business success. These factors—coupled with the need to align people directly with corporate goals—are forcing HR to evolve from policy creation, cost reduction, process efficiency, and risk management to driving a new talent mindset in the organization.

One important distinction is the evolution of the difference between tactical HR and strategic talent management. Transactional HR activities are administrative overhead. Talent management is a continuous process that delivers the optimal workforce for your business.

In this new model—instead of being the owners of processes, forms, and compliance— HR becomes the strategic enabler of talent management processes that empower managers and employees while creating business value.

With this view, talent management may be defined as the implementation of integrated strategies or systems designed to improve processes for recruiting, developing and retaining people with the required skills and aptitude to meet current and future organizational needs.

Anecdotally, talent management is often defined as performance management, incentive compensation, or talent acquisition. Talent management is also often confused with leadership development. Although leadership development is a crucial function of your organization, focusing on it exclusively is a legacy of last century. Our modern service and knowledge economies in the talent age require a broad and holistic view. A high performance business depends on a wide range of talent.

Taleo's graphical representation emphasizes the mandate of talent management to respond to business goals and consequently be the driver of business performance. Talent management is depicted as a circular—not a linear—set of activities.

Why Talent Management

Workforce cost is the largest category of spend for most organizations. Automation and analysis of your recruiting and hiring processes provides the immediate workforce visibility and insights you need to significantly improve your bottom line. Performance management provides the ongoing processes and practices to maintain a stellar workforce.

Today, many organizations are struggling with silos of HR processes and technologies. The future of talent management is embodied in solutions designed from the ground up to provide business-centric functionality on a unified talent management platform.

Since, nearly all competitive business factors have become commoditized, talent is what ultimately drives business success and creates value. Leading organizations rely on Taleo solutions and services to assess, acquire, develop, and align talent with business objectives while significantly reducing process costs, improving quality of hire, reducing risk, and achieving higher levels of performance.

Though it may seem intuitive, it is worthwhile to articulate the fundamental significance of successful talent management practices:

- The key enabler of any organization is talent.
- The quality of your people is your last true competitive differentiator.
- Talent drives performance.

Talent management requires strong executive support, along with systems and processes all directed towards having the right talent doing the right work at the right time. That's when talent truly drives higher business performance.

A global talent shortage is challenging firms worldwide to revamp their people management strategies—and Asian firms face bigger challenges than most.

According to the results of a recent Mercer survey, talent management is going to be a top priority for Asian firms over the next few years. Almost all the Asia Pacific respondents to the firm's *Future of Talent Management Survey* anticipate an increase in competition for the best employees over the next three to five years, with 53 per cent expecting that increase in competition to be significant.

And in the wake of the global financial crisis, firms across all industry verticals must revisit the strategies they use to attract, nurture and retain their key employees—or face a bleak future. "It's a different business environment now," says Jason Jeffay, Mercer's Global Leader of Talent Management Consulting. "We're looking ahead to a period of positive but slower growth, which translates into different talent needs. Talent programmes need to be reviewed and tailored to fit this new reality."

The findings are backed up by the results of a separate study conducted by recruitment specialists Manpower Group, in which the number of Asia Pacific employers reporting difficulty filling job vacancies due to lack of available talent stood at 45 per cent—well above the global average of 34 per cent. Japanese companies reported the most critical skills shortages, with four-out-of-five employers finding it difficult to hire staff with the right skills; meanwhile, two-thirds of companies in India, and 54 per cent in Australia and Taiwan, reported similar problems.

Peter Haglund, Country Manager of Manpower Singapore, said: "While not all employers are feeling the pain associated with the global talent shortage, external forces mean it is likely that they will soon feel pressure. Businesses need to adopt a long-term approach to ensuring they have the talent they need to achieve their business objectives."

As such, talent management programmes must be seen as key to addressing the talent shortage. "You can't manage what you can't measure," says Brenda Wilson, Mercer's Asia Pacific Leader of Talent Management Consulting. "Leading organizations have shown they are more effective at tailoring talent management practices to fit their own business models when taking a more quantitative, fact-based measurement approach. And we have found this approach steadily drives improvements year after year."

CHAPTER

9

Talent Management an Overview

*—Dr. Ch. Tirupathi Rao, M.Com., B.L., Ph.D.**

Talent management is a term that emerged in the 1990's to incorporate developments in Human Resources Management which placed more of an emphasis on the management of human resources or talent. The term was coined by David Watkins of Soft cape published in an article in 1998; however the connection between human resources development and organizational effectiveness has been established since the 1970's. Talent management is part of the Evolution of Talent Measurement Technologies.

The issue with many companies today is that their organizations put tremendous effort into attracting employees to their company, but spend little time into retaining and developing talent. A talent management system must be worked into the business strategy and implemented in daily processes throughout the company as a whole. It cannot be left solely to the human resources department to attract and retain employees, but rather must be practiced at all levels

*Reader in Commerce, Govt. Degree College (Men), Srikakulam-53001, Andhra Pradesh.

of the organization. The business strategy must include responsibilities for line managers to develop the skills of their immediate subordinates. Divisions within the company should be openly sharing information with other departments in order for employees to gain knowledge of the overall organizational objectives. Companies that focus on developing their talent integrate plans and processes to track and manage their employee talent, including the following:

- Sourcing, attracting, recruiting and onboarding qualified candidates with competitive backgrounds.
- Managing and defining competitive salaries.
- Training and development opportunities.
- Performance management processes.
- Retention programs.
- Promotion and transitioning.

The Talent Management strategy may be supported by technology such as HRIS (HR Information Systems) or HRMS (HR Management Systems). Modern techniques also use Competency-based management methodologies to capture and utilize competencies appropriate to strategically drive an organization's long-term plans.

Talent Management

It takes Talent to spot Talent! A tone deaf will never be able to appreciate the music of maestros. Only a seasoned jeweler would know that all that glitters is not real! And, only those who can recognize the worth of a diamond can value it, for others it's just a stone! Talent is doing easily what others find difficult.

In an organization, there is nothing more crucial than fitting the right employee in the right position. Or else you would be trying to fit a square peg in a round hole. When people do jobs that just don't suit their liking, inclination or temperament, the results, or rather the lack of them, will be disastrously obvious. Low productivity, dissatisfaction, low morale, absenteeism and other negative behaviour will become typical till the employee is shown the door. Or perhaps, there is another option—Talent Management.

Talent management implies recognizing a person's inherent skills, traits, personality and offering him a matching job. Every person has a unique talent that suits a particular job profile and any other position will cause discomfort.

It is the job of the Management, particularly the HR Department, to place candidates with prudence and caution. A wrong fit will result in further hiring, re-training and other wasteful activities.

No matter how inspiring the Leaders are, they are only as effective as their team. A team's output is healthy only if the members are in sync. To achieve such harmony, the key ingredient is "putting the right people in the right jobs".

While there is no magic formula to manage talent, the trick is to locate it and encourage it.

Talent Management is beneficial to both the organization and the employees. The organization benefits from: Increased productivity and capability; a better linkage between individuals' efforts and business goals; commitment of valued employees; reduced turnover; increased bench strength and a better fit between people's jobs and skills. Employees benefit from: Higher motivation and commitment; career development; increased knowledge about and contribution to company goals; sustained motivation and job satisfaction.

So, how does an organization effectively manage talent?

Recognize Talent: Notice what do employees do in their free time and find out their interests. Try to discover their strengths and interests. Also, encourage them to discover their own latent talents. For instance, if an employee in the operations department convincingly explains why he thinks he's right even when he's wrong, consider moving him to sales!

Attracting Talent: Good companies create a strong brand identity with their customers and then deliver on that promise. Great employment brands do the same, with quantifiable and qualitative results. As a result, the right people choose to join the organization.

Selecting Talent: Management should implement proven talent selection systems and tools to create profiles of the right people based on the competencies of high performers. It's not simply a matter of finding the "best and the brightest," it's about creating the right fit—both for today and tomorrow.

Retaining Talent: In the current climate of change, it's critical to hold onto the key people. These are the people who will lead the organization to future success, and you can't afford to lose them.

The cost of replacing a valued employee is enormous. Organizations need to promote diversity and design strategies to retain people, reward high performance and provide opportunities for development

Managing Succession: Effective organizations anticipate the leadership and talent requirement to succeed in the future. Leaders understand that it's critical to strengthen their talent pool through succession planning, professional development, job rotation and workforce planning. They need to identify potential talent and groom it.

Change Organisation Culture: Ask yourself, "Why would a talented person choose to work here?" If the organization wishes to substantially strengthen its talent pool, it should be prepared to change things as fundamental as the business strategy, the organization structure, the culture and even the caliber of leaders in the organization.

A rightly managed talent turns out to be a Gold Mine. It's inexhaustible and priceless. It will keep supplying wealth and value to the organization.

In turn, Management needs to realize its worth, extract it, polish it and utilize it. Don't hoard Talent—spend it lavishly, like a millionaire flashing his luxuries, because Talent is Wealth!

Talent Management is a Business Problem

Talent Management describes the process through which employers of all kinds—firms, government, non-profits—anticipate their human capital needs and set about meeting them. Getting the right people with the right skills into the right jobs, a common definition of talent management, is the basic people Management challenge in organizations. While the focus of Talent Management tends to be on Management and executive positions, the issues apply to all jobs that are hard to fill.

Decisions about Talent Management shape the competencies that organizations have and their ultimate success, and from the perspective of individuals, these decisions determine the path and pace of careers. Talent Management practices can have a crucial impact on society as well. The lifetime employment model of the post-WWII generation, for example, provided the economic stability that created middle class society.

Failures in Talent Management may be more recognizable than the concept itself. Those failures mean mismatches between supply and demand: Too many employees, leading to layoffs and restructurings on the one hand, and not enough talent, leading to talent crunches on the other. In India at present, it may be hard to imagine the problem of having too much talent, but the first downturn in the economy- or even in a section of the economy—will make that clear. These mismatches are among the fundamental problems that businesses and other large employers face. Over the past generation, corporations in particular seem to have lurched from surpluses of talent to shortfalls to surpluses and back to shortfalls again. The challenge employers face is to track much more closely the demands for talent to avoid both shortfalls and oversupplies.

Many observers assume that the Management of talent is really about the internal development of human capital, yet the majority of vacancies in corporations now are filled from outside. They also assume that internal development practices such as executive coaching, career pathing developmental assignments, assessment centers, high potential programmes, and succession planning, are something new.

These techniques and indeed, every employee development practice that seems novel now—forced ranking performance evaluation systems, 360 degree feedback programmes, executive coaching, etc.—were all common in the 1950s. Except at a few very large firms, they have been scaled back and, in many cases, largely abandoned. The reason was not that these practices failed to develop talent. It was because they were too costly. And the biggest cost was the difficulty they faced in managing the unpredictability of the demand for talent.

Internal development of talent collapsed in the 1970s when business forecasting failed to predict the downturn in the economy, and the talent pipelines continued to turn out talent under the forecast assumptions of booming corporate growth. The excess supply of talent and the no-layoff policies for white collar workers caused a bloating of corporate organizations, and the steepness of the 1981 recession in the US and elsewhere led virtually all companies to back away from developing talent. Lifetime employment came to an end, and the reengineering processes cut away the development practices and staff that created talent. After all, if the priority was to get rid of talent, why would companies maintain the programmes designed to create it.

We need a new way of thinking about the talent management challenge. A new framework for Talent Management has to begin by being clear about the goal. Talent Management is not an end in itself. It is not about developing employees or creating succession plans. Nor is it about achieving specific benchmarks like a five per cent turnover rate, having the most educated workforce, or any other tactical outcome. The goal of Talent Management is the much more general but important task of helping the organization achieve its overall objectives. In the business world, that objective is to make money.

An important part of the goal of helping the organization is to address the financial challenge associated with developing employees and recouping the investments in their development now that labour markets:

The cost of employing those workers in the initial period exceeds the value of the contribution from them as the new hires are learning what to do and how to do it. The size of the cost gap grows as development efforts expand. That investment has historically been recouped in the next period, in the shaded blue area where the value an employee produces exceeds the cost of employing them. Even though wages and employment costs are rising, the value of the employee's contribution rises even faster, and the employer earns back a return on their earlier investment. As long as the gap between costs and contributions is bigger in this second period than in the first, then the employer makes money on the investment. At the end of an individual's career, pension plans and other retirement programmes reversed the flow of resources. During that period, the employer makes net payments back to the employees.

The problem with this approach to recouping development costs began soon after the collapse of lifetime employment for managers and executives. As described in Chapter 2, employers broke that model first by laying off experienced employees. But layoffs alone did not necessarily collapse the ability to earn a return on training and development. That happened when employers began hiring experienced talent from competitors, in part at the executive level as a means for changing the strategy and culture of their own organizations but then later as a means of avoiding the time delays and costs associated with internal development.

The flip side of hiring experienced workers is retention problems for competitors. The situation is sometimes described as an "incomplete contract"—the employer makes an investment in the employee but did not require anything in return because, historically, the employee had little opportunity to leave. Once outside hiring started, an employee's competencies became useful elsewhere and had a market value. In fact, an employee may actually be more valuable to a competitor than to their current employer because they bring with them not only their own performance but knowledge and insight about how their old employer operated.

The competitors can pay the employee more than the current employer and still make money on the deal because they have no early investment costs to recoup. In the graph above, the market value of the employee becomes something closer to the line representing their true value to an employer. Employers then face what seems like an impossible choice: Either stay with their practices and watch their newly developed employees leave for better paying opportunities elsewhere, losing their investment in them, or raise wages up to the new market level, losing the ability to recoup the investments they have just made in their employees.

What we need to address going forward is how to make investments in development affordable, and part of that challenge involves employee retention, making it possible to at least retain employees long enough to recoup the training investments in them.

Research on Talent Management

HR directors see talent mobility as a growing priority for the next 12 months, according to recent research. However, a low level of sophistication in talent management systems has hampered the introduction of a mobility strategy. A report revealed exclusively to HR magazine reveals nearly a quarter (22%) of HR decision-makers expect to see an increase in voluntary churn in 2011, highlighting this as a major threat to business growth over the next year. According to Taleo's *Talent Mobility in 2011* research, which surveyed 500 HR decision-makers in large UK companies, increased churn was highlighted as a particular concern for business services (32%), public sector (28%) and IT/technology companies (27%). However, while HR decision-makers identified this as a concern for 2011, the majority attributed retention problems to external factors, such as better salaries (48%) or opportunities (45%) elsewhere, as opposed to internal factors.

The recent research highlighted that talent mobility is increasingly on the HR agenda for 2011, with 71 per cent of respondents agreeing that it is important for companies to be able to proactively and strategically move people from role to role. However, the extent to which companies are moving people within their businesses effectively remains limited, with many citing a number of recurring barriers, which they believe are preventing them from achieving a truly mobile workforce.

The top three barriers to talent mobility were identified as; lack of visibility into talent gaps and opportunities; lack of systems/technology to support talent mobility initiatives; and quality and reliability of employee talent data. A low level of sophistication in terms of talent mobility technology emerged as a particular barrier for the majority of organizations, limiting the ability of HR professionals and senior management to identify where the opportunities and gaps within their organization lie and matching these with existing, internal skill sets.

Overall, only one in ten (10%) of the companies surveyed were using dedicated talent management systems, with the use of dedicated systems proving higher in the construction/ manufacturing (14%) and IT/technology (14%) sectors. The majority of companies reported they were still 'making do' with company intranets to facilitate internal mobility, and in 30 per cent of cases, companies were still relying solely on email to facilitate internal mobility.

Alice Snell, VP research at Taleo, said: "As many organizations plan for growth in 2011, and confidence in the job market returns, employees who may have chosen to sit tight over the past few years are likely to begin exploring new opportunities, seeking new roles and new challenges.

"However, introducing an effective talent mobility strategy, which allows companies to mobilize people internally in response to business needs can not only make great business sense, but can prove an excellent retention tool, offering employees internal opportunities to develop their career with their current employer.

"The value of a talent mobility strategy is clearly recognized among the HR profession. However, it is currently being thwarted by a number of factors, most notably easily corrected system and data shortcomings. While the use of technology to support mobility is currently limited, evidence suggests that there are notable business benefits associated with a more sophisticated level of technology usage, from boosting the leadership pipeline to being better able to drive change and business growth. The companies that will be best placed to meet future challenges as we return to economic growth will be those that have the processes, systems and culture in place to support a holistic approach to talent mobility."

Global Talent Management Systems

LAS VEGAS—"Think global efficiency; act local in responsiveness." That was the advice given by Rick Fletcher when HR professionals choose and implement a global talent Human Resource Information Systems (HRIS) management system. Fletcher, president of HR chitect, a Frisco, Texas-based human capital management systems consulting firm, spoke at a March 20 concurrent session at the 29th annual

Society for Human Resource Management Global Forum Conference & Exposition here.

An increasing number of vendors are providing global staffing systems that achieve this global-local balance with a "transnational" approach rather than a multinational, international or "mega-national" one, Fletcher said. The latter three, which are used by most global companies currently, are effective either locally or globally—not both. He encouraged attendees to look for a global talent management system that accomplishes both goals.

Transnational solutions are more robust and scalable to meet future growth, and they enable each locality to maintain unique operations while following and supporting global resourcing policies, principles and processes, Fletcher explained. Thus, maintaining local needs doesn't come at the expense of meeting harmonized global objectives.

Vendors providing transnational talent systems are moving toward a "talent management suite" solution that bundles applicant tracking software, employee performance management and incentive compensation systems—giving users a one-stop shop for staffing needs. The leading vendors are Authoria, Kenexa and Soft cape, said Fletcher.

An emerging trend in this space is providing solutions for the mid-size market. "There is an untapped market of about 40,000 mid-size U.S. companies that are expanding globally," he said, "presenting a huge opportunity for a vendor to fill."

Still, the transnational global talent management system comes at a higher cost. In addition, companies may encounter some system implementation and adoption issues if proper selection and deployment methods aren't followed, he said. And companies may have to customize the system further to meet local legal compliance mandates.

This makes vendor selection and project implementation strategy very important to gaining the most return on investment with transnational global talent management systems, said Fletcher.

Selecting a Vendor

Before embarking on the vendor selection journey, HR needs to do some preparation in-house. First, define the project's scope, costs and budget fully. "This is the No. 1 risk mitigation factor in the success of implementing a global talent management system," said Fletcher.

Next, put the right global project team together. Select stakeholders from all major global regions, countries and business functions—HR, IT, procurement and communications, Fletcher suggested. Finally, define your global talent management strategy and conduct a thorough requirements study through surveys of users. This preparation will save a lot of headaches down the road, he said.

U.S. companies looking to select a global talent management system also need to consider the following, said Fletcher:

- **Language:** Make sure that the vendor can accommodate country and regional dialects of the users and candidates.
- **Legal issues:** The applicant tracking system needs to track required data and ensure compliance. For instance, "definition of an applicant" changes are occurring in countries outside the United States. In addition, privacy laws follow the employee across borders. So, employee data are subject to the privacy laws of the country of which they are citizens—not the country in which they are working.
- **Cultural issues:** Local cultures hold differences on such issues as ethnicity, gender, nationality and religion—which impact the data needed to be tracked. HR also needs to consider the a Iture's inclination toward new technologies.

- **Technological matters:** A wide range exists on the access to the Internet at home and at work in various countries. Fewer than 5 per cent in China and India have access to the web, compared to nearly half in Australia and Scandinavian countries. Implementation tips

Before implementing a new global talent management system, you must gather global team members for an in-person meeting. "This is an expense up front, but it will pay off for you in the long-run," said Fletcher. "You will build trust and get buy-in, and I have found all my successful implementations started with an in-face meeting."

This team should include the players involved in the selection as well as a senior executive at the talent management system vendor. "I also suggest you get a 'problem user' involved on the implementation team—someone who really liked the old system and is showing resistance to change," Fletcher said. "That person will end up being your best leader when he returns home."

Create a global implementation project plan. Identify the country with the most complex needs and pilot the system there first. That will reveal kinks and allow time to work them out before going live globally, Fletcher explained.

Communication is the second risk mitigation factor in implementing a global talent management system successfully, he said. Use the technology vehicles appropriate to the individual locales. It's important to get buy-in and to provide support after implementation, said Fletcher.

Industry Consolidation

With the growing trend of offering a complete talent management suite, applicant tracking providers are buying out performance management system providers and *vice versa* to become best-of-breed vendors,

In addition, large enterprise resource planning vendors, such as Oracle, SAP and Lawson, are improving their talent management system components, but they have not caught up with talent Management system best-of-breed vendors, said Fletcher.

Companies are reducing the number of vendor suppliers and embracing the suite concept. However, "there are too many suppliers for demand," Fletcher said, indicating that the consolidation of vendors will speed up.

"You have to consider if the vendor will be around in the next two years," said Fletcher. *Adrienne Fox is managing editor of HR* Magazine.

Get Real Value from your Talent Management Practices

What if you could align, develop and leverage the potential of every employee in your company? And confidently lead executive discussions and decision-making on a host of workforce and talent management issues? Getting control of your most important strategic asset—your workforce—is easier and more affordable than you think.

Thousands of HR professionals around the world are using Halogen talent management solutions with brilliant results. You can too.

Product Tour;

Be confident. Be strategic. Be brilliant at Talent Management!

Talent Management Best-Practices at Your Fingertips.

Halogen provides powerful, market leading talent management solutions that follow industry best practices. Yet they are breathtakingly easy to implement and use, making it simple for you to:

- Align employee and organizational goals, giving everyone visibility and accountability for success;
- Give employees the richly-detailed performance appraisals they need to develop and succeed, including 360 degree feedback.

- Easily identify skill gaps, assign targeted development plans to address them, and measure their effectiveness in terms of increased performance.
- Link learning and development programmes to bottom line success.
- Know who your top performers are and groom them as part of your succession planning.
- Recognize employee contributions with pay for performance compensation management.
- Manage job descriptions and integrate them with all your talent management processes, ensuring every employee knows their current job responsibilities and clearly understand what's expected of them.
- Align and integrate talent acquisition with your overall talent management strategy.
- Monitor your talent management processes and get critical workforce data with easy to read, real-time dashboards and reports.

Halogen makes it easy to take full control of your talent management processes. In fact, you can do things "your way" at any time without having to rely on the vendor - or breaking the bank. Automate your time-consuming, paper-based talent management processes and drive accountability and consistency—all while reducing your administrative burden.

Choose to purchase just the modules you need today, and easily add new ones tomorrow. Plus, you can take advantage of as many of the features each module offers as you want; you'll never have to "upgrade" to a different version of our software to accommodate growth or implement more sophisticated functionality. Our proven implementation programmes and customized training will get you up and running and self-sufficient in as short a time as possible. And we back them all with our Certain to Succeed Money Back Guarantee. That's brilliant—and you will be too!

Most organizations today understand the significance of their human capital and the value of connecting their talent strategy to meet business objectives. Talent Management Systems focus on providing strategic assistance to organizations in the accomplishment of long-term enterprise goals with respect to talent or human capital.

The challenge facing most organizations is in keeping track of all the personnel data such as employee contact details, present skill sets, leaves, sick time, vacation, emergency contact, etc. and making changes to it in real-time.

Kensium Talent Management System will assist your organization in developing, managing, rewarding and optimizing your organizational talent to increase workforce productivity and maximize operating performance.

Kensium Talent Management System offers a flexible and easy to use solution for companies of all sizes. By providing modules for personal information management, employee self-service, leave, time & attendance, benefits and recruitment, companies are able to manage their crucial organization asset - people. The combination of these modules into one application assures the perfect platform for re-engineering and aligning your HR processes with organizational goals.

Our solutions can easily be tailored to meet the unique needs and business objectives of organizations in every major industry vertical.

CHAPTER

10

Talent Utilization in India

Some Reflections

*—Dr. B.Eswar Rao Pattnaik**

Introduction

Creativity and talent of people of a country are the harbingers of Development. Education is a key element in any Nations Development. The universal Declaration of human rights by U.N.O. asserts that "Every one has the right or Education." The enactment of right of children to free and compulsory education by the Government of India in 2009 makes it the obligations of the Central Government and State Government for providing free and compulsory education to every child between the age of Six and fourteen. There are three aspects of education in a Country (1) knowledge creation (2) knowledge utilization (3) Knowledge diffusion. Literacy is a right in itself because, without it people do not have equal life chances & opportunities. One bright spot in the body of education sector in India is it's literacy rate of people that is 68.4 per cent. Female literacy rate is less promising (53.7%) in the country.

---

*Retired Reader in Economics S.B.R.G. Women's College, Berhampur, Orissa.

Importance of Education

1. Amartya Sen argues that education can add to a person's effective in freedom.
2. Education has an instrumental role for a person as it enables a person to get a job.
3. Education improves collective demands for social security and health care.
4. Formal education prevents child labour by encouraging school enrolment.
5. The weaker section of societies will resist oppression by organizing itself politically.

Progress in Education Sector

In Indian economy has marched on the path of quantitative expansion in education.

The no. of schools & colleges have gone up impressively from 0.23 million and 370 in 1950-51 to 1.28 million and 11698 in 2005-06 respectively. There has been a quantum jump in the no. of professional colleges and universities from 208 and 27 in 1950-51 to 7797 and 350 in 2005-06 respectively. It is heartening to note that, there has been an appreciable increase in Gross enrolment Ratio in Elementary education from 32:1 per cent 2005-06 to 94.85 per cent in 2005-06. Today, there is one primary school in every village within radius of 1 km.

However, pockets still exist in many, remote parts of the country where the nearly secondary school or college is too far from the village. The Government's expenditure on education is 3 per cent G.D.P. far below 6 per cent norm recommended by Radhakrishan Commission long ago. There is also gender gap in literary performance. Tribal & S.C population, physically challenged persons and people living from low social and economic status have access to education of lower quality than others. The recent focus of public authorities is on inclusive education to the disadvantageous sections of society, so that, they can catch up with the rest.

Yaspal, the noted educationist observes that "A university should aspire the function of combining knowledge with that of creating new knowledge. There should be an atmosphere enveloping the whole university space that everything is not known, that "There is enormous amount waiting for those who would develop discerning eyes—for phenomenon, for relationships for ways of discovering what lies beyond the current horizon. Such an atmosphere should pervade most departments, schools, centers & even administration. It is desirable that vice chancellors of universities should have personally tasted creativity.

Knowledge is like, a tree and there should be an interdisciplinary approach to different subjects like Arts, Science, Biology, Physics, Economics and Commerce. Yashpal, head of the committee set up by HRD Ministry to advice on Rennovation & Rejuvenation of Higher Education counsels that the UGC and AICTE should be subsumed, within a single Higher Education Commission. It is healthy to set up world Class University & like Massachusetts (M.I.T.) Institute of Technology, which is engaged with a wide range of knowledge, both at under graduate and graduate level. The M.I.T. simultaneously conducts worlds class programmes in Science, Astronomy, Management, Language, comparative literature, philosophy, psychology, IT. law, political science, economics, agriculture and such emerging disciplines, Autonomy of colleges and Universities should be respected with minimum necessary interference and inspection in this functioning. Colleges should be self regulating partners in managing their institutions subject is monitoring & inspections by appropriate bodies.

Aligning Higher Educations with the Labour Market

There should be easy transfers for vocational studies to academic stream and there should be no stigma in taking vocational course. Pawan Agarwal (2009) argues that, introduction of two year associate degree with focus on vocational skills through the existing polytechnics and general Arts and Science colleges would go a long way in aligning education with the labour market. Higher economic growth accomplished by the economy in recent years has created demand for new jobs in I.T. pharmaceuticals biotechnology, aviation, hospitality, medical, retail trade, real estate, banking; insurance, hospitality and infrastructure. Proper man power planning in these spheres like incentives for migration & skill formation may overcome of skilful labour in these sectors.

(A.I.M.) Management Techniques

G. Narayan, vadora based management expert has developed appropriate integrated management (A.I.T.) for modern problems. The tenet involves learning by example and focuses on time honoured sama, (Persuasion) Dana (reward), Bheda (Discriminations) and danda (Punishment). AIM Technique can be applied differently in cases of sattvic (knowledge oriented) person, Rajasik (ego-oriented) persons and tamasic (ignorance oriented) persons, to as observed by Times of India (08.09.2010). It involves there way approach to transactional analysis, child, the adult and the parent-the Bhagavadgita visualizes a four way approach child, youth, adult and the elder.

Emotional Intelligence

Salovey and Mayer (1990) have developed the concept of emotional intelligence. It was Daniel Goleman who has popularized emotional intelligence construct in 1990, in his ground breaking book emotional intelligence: Why it can matter more than IQ in 1995.

Emotional intelligence has been defined as “the capacity for recognizing ones for own feeling and those of others emotions for motivating ourselves and in our relationships.

Goleman's model identities four main emotional intelligence constructs such as, self-awareness, self-management, social awareness and relationship management. With a set of emotional competencies within each construct. The first construct self-awareness denotes the ability to know one's internal states, preferences, resources, intuition and forms the foundation for self-confidence. The second construct, self-management entails controlling one's emotions and impulses and adapting to changing circumstances. The third construct, social awareness, means the ability to sense understand and reacting to other's emotions while comprehending social networks. Relationship management, the fourth construct involves the ability to inspire, influence and develop others, while managing conflict.

Suggestion

Peter Drucker observes succinctly Efficiency is doing things right; effectiveness is doing the right things. The Bhagavad Gita notes "yogah karmasu Kausalam (skill in action is yoga). Talent refers to physical, mentaland emotional faculties, of a person along, with aptitude for specific works. Talent is at once an inherent quality of a person and also is stimulated by external factors like, education, training , skill up-gradation, migration, dignity of labour, goal orientation, hard work, innovation, communicative and skills, motivation, cultural exchanges between industries, seminar awards and Promotions for better performance.

Accounting Procedures and industrial, rules and regulations, too should be transparent in a country to enable the blossoming of enterprise. The proposals for setting up of an industry should get quick clearance by Government. In recent years the Government has enacted a law to regulate entry of Foreign Education providers. A law to establish a Tribunal to fast-track adjudication of disputes concerning stake holders (teachers students, employees and management) is proposed in higher education. In school education, it is proposed to evolve a system of Public-Private Partnership Efforts should be made to encourage I.C.T. in secondary schools and in open distance schooling through broadband connectivity. Remedial coaching for students hailing from S.C & S.T population will be provided. Academic reforms include, choice based credit system. Semester, regular revision of syllabus, impetus to research etc. Broadband internet connectivity will be provided in 5000 colleges and universities.

Conclusion

To conclude, creativity is possible when mind is empty and not crowded with, through just as a vessel is full, when it is empty. What is needed, is a silent, watchful and open mind, that is free from likes and dislikes and observes facts and events of life dispassionately and objectively.

REFERENCES

1. Several Dailies of Timely of India.
2. J.K. Krishna Murthy *"Freedom from the known"*.
3. Yashpal *"Management of Universities"* September 2009.
4. Pawan Agarwal *"Aligning Higher Education with the Labour Market"* Yojana Sep. 2009.
5. "Shashak Chaturvedi *"Challenges before Education in India"*, Yojana, Sep. 2009.
6. S. Chandra Sekhar and Krishna Priya "The Emotionally Intelligent Teacher, Yojana, Sep. 2009.
7. B. Eswar Rao Pattnaik. *"Plan Performances in Education & Health Sectors in Orissa in social sector development in India,* Raj Kumar Sen (ED), Deep & Deep Publications Ltd.
8. Jean Dreze Amartaya Sen, *India Economic Development and Social Opportunity,* Oxford India Paperbacks.

CHAPTER

11

Talent Management after Globalisation

*—G. Chandrayya**

Introduction

We're in a talent crisis that is growing in intensity. The global talent war is upon us. As organizations struggle to find, retain, motivate, and develop their people adequately, they face an ever-dynamic talent landscape that is more globally competitive, demanding, and expensive than ever before. Adding to the challenge are growing numbers of aging retired candidates, shifting business requirements, and attractive competing job offers that keep executives and HR professionals up at night. America's largest 500 companies will lose 50 per cent of their senior managers in the next five years, according to RHR International. And a survey by the Society for Human Resource Management said that 83 per cent of workers were likely to search for a new job in the coming couple of years. But this aging of the talent base and restless workforce are just two of the forces impacting today's

*G. Chandrayya, Senior Lecturer, Department of Commerce, Government College, Rajahmundry, East Godavari District, A.P.

talent war. Fundamental and rapid changes in the world economy, coupled with strong economic growth, are making it far more difficult for companies to adequately address their need for talent and growth.

Talent management is increasingly a part of the corporate strategy for most organizations.You don't have to look very far to see articles about attracting, developing, and retaining talent. Forecasts abound on retirements, labour shortages, quality of new hires, and lack of future leaders. All point to the need for organizations to act now or risk losing competitive advantage. To maintain a competitive advantage and to meet the demands of business, organizations need to identify, select, and develop their employees in a way that both supports the company's business goals and provides employees with a clear career path. In other words, organizations must become deliberate and strategic in their programmes for managing their talent. Presents the key terms, concepts, and practices related to talent management. Examines in depth each stage in the talent management life cycle, from talent acquisition to retirement. This article will quickly outline the competencies of top executives at startups today, and the high level of innovation and creativity required amongst HR practitioners seeking to attract and retain top talent to drive the success of nascent organizations in a globalizing Indian environment.

Key Functions of A Talent Management

(*a*) Toolset, Assessment (Ongoing);

(*b*) Business Objective Orientation (Task Relevance);

(*c*) Performance Appraisal/Review;

(*d*) Talent Requirements;

(*e*) Talent Pool Development and Management, (Referrals, Direct Marketing, Sourcing);

(*f*) Recruiting, Internal Rotation.

Features of Talent Management

(1) Attracting and retaining enough employees at all levels to meet the needs of organic and inorganic growth,

(2) Creating a value proposition that appeals to multiple generations. With four generations in today's workplace, most companies are struggling to create an employee experience that appeals to individuals with diverse needs,

(3) Preferences and assumptions,

(4) Developing a robust leadership pipeline,

(5) Rounding out the capabilities of hires who lack the breadth of necessary for global leadership,

(6) Transferring key knowledge and relationships,

(7) Stemmmg the exodus of Gen X'ers from corporate life,

(8) Redesigning talent management practices to attract and retain Gen Y's.

(9) Creating a workplace that is open to Boomers in their "second careers,"

(10) Overcoming a "norm" of short tenure and frequent movement,

(11) Enlisting executives who don't appreciate the challenge,

(12) Attracting and keeping the Best People Indicators of Best Talent Management:

Competency Gap Index: This is the difference between the skills the organization needs to achieve its goals, and those that its current workforce possesses. Most skill gaps can be corrected through the implementation of comprehensive training programmes, or by using talent management software to realign employee roles and responsibilities based on individual strengths. However, major skill gaps can be detrimental to productivity and may require drastic measures such as headcount replacements or a complete restructuring of organizational charts.

Employee Satisfaction Index: How happy are employees in their current jobs, and how likely are they to leave? It is important to note that measuring the satisfaction index alone is not enough. Companies need to use their talent management system to understand the underlying causes behind high levels of dissatisfaction, so corrective action can be taken to minimize attrition.

Workforce Confidence Index: This indicator assesses employee perceptions of the abilities of the organization as a whole. Do workers believe that the company and its staff are well-prepared to execute on important plans and achieve strategic goals? Unlike the employee satisfaction index, which measures each individual's opinion of their specific job, this metric provides insight into the reputation of the organization among its workforce.

Ratio of External: Hires to Internal Promotions. When high-level positions open up, companies should be able to find candidates internally before turning to external searches. However, this is not always the case, as few companies have fully leveraged their talent management strategies to develop and implement comprehensive advancement plans. This metric serves as a "wake up call", helping companies to understand if they are properly cultivating their existing talent. The most vital talent management metrics will vary greatly from one organization to the next, depending upon unique plans and goals. The key is to be sure that they are clear and well-defined, as well as easy to track and measure, and actionable. It is also important to communicate the results to stakeholders throughout the organization, so everyone knows whether or not talent management objectives are being met. Additionally, benchmarking progress against other companies in the same industry can provide even more insight into how well an organization is doing.

Time Tested Models of Talent Management

Skill & Competency Models

The development and planned use of competency tools is essential for recruitment, growth, promotion and retention. Competency tools should reflect uniform, values-based expectations of employees, such as trust, contribution, productivity and team work, as well as position-based knowledge, skills and abilities.

Workforce Metrics

Understanding functional measurement fundamentals requires that institutions: Understand the business case for measurement develop a common language associated with measurement. Understand leading and lagging metrics and the value of each. Learn the taxonomy of measurement and what measures match best with needed reporting. Understand balanced scorecards and be able to adapt those to unit reporting. Examine institutional strategies and how to link unit plans to those strategies. Set outcome based, measurable targets for value-added contribution. Determine the metrics that will demonstrate success in terms of quality, quantity, cost, time, communication and customer satisfaction.

Strategic Workforce Planning

Strategic Workforce Planning (SWP) system enables institutions to better understand future talent requirements, anticipate and address talent gaps before they have a negative organizational impact, and more effectively prioritize and implement the actions required to ensure the right people are in the right place at the right time. Why consider Strategic Workforce Planning? Making uninformed choices around current and future talent requirements can significantly restrict an institution's ability to execute its strategy. Traditional approaches to workforce planning have proven to be woefully inadequate as they do not provide the insights, analytics or information needed to. Clearly link institution strategy to human capital needs—Identify the specific number, type and quality of talent required to execute on your strategy, SWP is a proven approach to more effectively Identify the type of talent required by your strategy.

Performance Profiling

Performance is a time saving collection of tools that integrates the complete evaluation process to include job profiling competency management, assessment reviews, objective setting and development plan creation. With Performance your organization easily creates and delivers more effective and insightful performance reviews, which result in enhanced communication and a more productive workforce. Produce quality reviews rapidly with significantly reduced paperwork. Assess talent bench strength for important business decisions, Identify skill gaps and plan for development; Enhance communication between employees, managers; and human resources professionals; Align employee objectives with business objectives provide online access globally.

Profile of Successful Entrepreneurs

A focus on an executive's mindset, as it relates to their technical and managerial skills, will unveil characteristics that are mission-critical for startups compared to more established companies. Without these traits, otherwise sound and capable executives are rendered completely ineffective in a startup environment. While during the initial stages of operation the cultures of one startup will be quite similar to another, over time they will become more differentiated as the businesses mature, requiring senior managers who embody the corporate ethos.

Attracting and Keeping the Best People

Many startups believe that they are in competition with established big brand companies for the best people, which is often an erroneous assumption. In fact, the profile described above of people who aspire to join startups are vastly different from those who want to be part of an established big brand company. In fact, the real competition is from other startups with the ability to attract and retain these potential candidates.

Survey on Trends, Challenges, Priorities, Successes

In order to study the issues affecting companies in their struggle to keep their talent competitive, the Business Performance Management Forum and Success Factors in co-operation with the Human Capital Institute conducted a survey of more than 725 performance and HR professionals. The 2007 Performance and Talent Management Trend Survey is a year-end audit and assessment of talent management trends and trajectories for 2007. This benchmark study examines the critical issues impacting businesses in their effort to remain competitive by acquiring, sustaining and managing talent across the enterprise.

Key Findings of the Study

(*a*) Increasing competition for talent is universal respondents say competition for talent is increasing in their industry, Talent costs this year are inflated. The cost of acquiring and keeping talent rose in 2006, and two thirds say to a somewhat or high degree.

(*b*) Talent management leaders are achieving significant benefits in a short period of time. Companies that have adopted advanced solutions for improving performance and talent management have done so in as little as a month, and are reaping the benefits in the form of dramatically reduced turnover, improved goal alignment, and better engaged and performing employees. Most companies, though, are way behind and playing talent management catch-up.

(c) Organizations point to an increasing influence of globalization and easing of business boundaries as having a profound effect on talent consideration. 77 per cent of all survey participants say that global factors. "Firms are realizing that money is only one factor. Having access to training and development, as well as creating an appropriate culture, are key. Being more flexible and adjusting to peoples' various schedules are essential. Managers need to be increasingly aware of things like this and be prepared to make adjustments accordingly."

(*d*) Talent Management is Top of Mind: Respondents overwhelmingly said that talent management is a strategic corporate focus. There is a growing concern and emphasis upon developing, engaging, and harnessing the potential of the company talent pool to drive further growth, success, and sustainability. Three quarters of participants said that talent management is a high or very high priority, and over one quarter gave talent management the highest priority rating on the scale.

(*e*) Critical Talent Competencies Changing Dramatically: Intelligence and Creativity of Little Value Organizations across the board are realizing that there has been a seismic shift in the skills and talents required to run their business and remain competitive. This is adding significant challenges to companies in high growth mode that must adapt to the changing talent landscape. 88 per cent of respondents stated that critical competencies are changing or evolving in their organization. And nearly half of participants said this change is to a high or very high degree.

(*f*) Talent War Intensifying: Companies See Need to Find, Develop, Engage, Measure, Keep Strong Staff Poll participants cited a wide range of talent management hurdles on the horizon for the new year. Top among them was the need to develop internal talent, followed closely by talent retention and turnover and talent acquisition. Employee engagement and performance evaluation ranked highly as well, underscoring the need to measure the internal workforce and keep them connected.

(*g*) Nearly everybody notes that competition for talent is heating up to some degree. This talent struggle is having a marked impact on the number of organizations that need to pay higher salaries, search longer for staff and implement better internal talent development. Many say that they need to settle for inferior employees, less flexible business models, and poor customer satisfaction.

(*h*) Rapid Corporate Growth and Change Driving Talent Acquisition Needs: Surprisingly, traditional reasons for acquiring talent have succumbed to a new set of drivers. Things like company growth, evolving internal cultures and changing market demands topped the list. Much less prominent were things like employee retirement, lagging loyalty, and poor employee performance.

(*i*) Workforces Gone Global; Big Business Feels the Effects: The rapid globalization of business and the expanding role of an international workforce are having a significant impact on how companies acquire and manage talent. As organizations look for new people and foster new skill sets, they need to take into account the challenges and opportunities posed by a more global outlook.

(*j*) When we look at small businesses, however, the story is different. Nearly a third of these companies said globalization does not have any impact on securing and nurturing talent.

(*k*) Most Don't Even Measure, Much Less Manage, Talent Effectively: Despite the need for better talent development, acquisition strategies and talent management processes, two out of three organizations don't have a talent scorecard in place. The old phrase "What gets measured gets done" is appropriate here, as effective talent optimization relies heavily on the ability to measure success.

(*l*) Rest Plans Aren't Laid Yet Small Business Exposed. Not only do most companies not have talent management metrics in place, but a significant don't have formal plans in place to identify, grow, and retain talent. For a shocking number when you consider that nearly all of the small businesses polled are in service-related industries where people are critical to the success of the business.

(*m*) Excerpts From The Experts: Through a set of consistent questions, we've gathered valuable additional insights regarding the priorities, challenges, and progress in talent acquisition and management. The results from the executive dialogs revealed that due to an intensifying competition for talent, there are huge benefits to implementing effective performance and talent management solutions. In particular, executives pointed to the following common trends.

(*n*) But wherever there is a challenge, there is also an opportunity. Better companies will further distance themselves from the pack by out-performing the competition in attracting, retaining and developing their talent. Indeed, our respondents said they viewed the increase of competition for talent as an opportunity to create competitive advantage through better talent management practices. As mentioned earlier in this report, that belief is supported by other recent research by Success Factors and human capital expert reveals that smarter human capital management leads to better financial performance.

(*o*) Organizations Putting More Emphasis on Effective Talent Management. It's no wonder that two-thirds of the executives participating in this study said their organizations consider talent management to be a high or very high strategic priority. Innovative organizations—in particular large companies—are catching on to the talent management wave. With more advanced and sophisticated technology, tools and processes at their disposal and the nagging need to improve talent management practices; these leaders will not remain idle.

A New Talent Management Framework: The concept of "Integrated Talent Management" became popular around five years ago—and since then organizations have used this phrase to describe an integrated approach to recruiting, development, performance management, compensation, development planning, and learning.

Integrated Talent Management

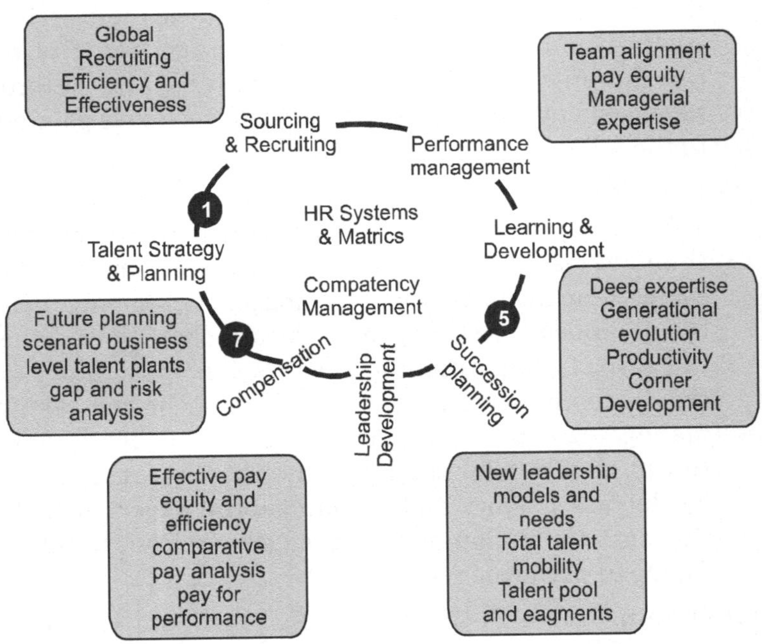

As this colourful model shows, many of the original concepts remain the same—but we have carefully added some new elements and reworded several functions to show how this whole area has evolved. First the concept of "sourcing and recruiting" has been expanded to use the term *"Talent Acquisition."* This enormous area has become very complex and highly interconnected today; organizations must assess critical talent needs, determine performance profiles, source and screen candidates, and then hire and onboard people. This whole area (which we are dedicating a new research library to) now touches the entire people-management process: head count and job requisitions must be included in the dynamic workforce plan, organizations must recruit internally as well as externally; job profiles and candidate information must be imported and stored in the talent systems; new people must go through a well-developed on boarding process; candidate quality should be checked against performance measures to help improve sources and recruiting process, compensation plans should be checked against existing plans, and the list goes on.

Note that we added *"Career Management"* to the core. Organizations now realize that the problems of performance management, development planning, succession management, talent mobility, and leadership development must include a formal and transparent process to help people build their own careers. One of our research members just told me this week that their turnover rates are starting to rise and their engagement levels are low—partly due to the stress of the recession. They quickly realized that the company had very little career development focus and one of her priorities for the next year is to build a career management programme, and associated management tools and training, for each major functional. In this new area we discuss the need to understand the broad portfolio of skills, knowledge, experience, and internal sources of information needed to drive success.

Workforce Planning: It is described in detail in our research. We consistently see that companies with 3 or 4 years of experience in integrated talent management then migrate their energy toward business-driven workforce planning. HP, for example, has developed a workforce planning process which asks each line manager to develop an ROI model for each hire. This model is built on the company's existing knowledge about the financial return and performance of different individuals in different roles. The goal of workforce planning is to move beyond the concept of an integrated set of headcount and open requisitions and integrate the process right into the annual business plan.

Talent strategy and business alignment: If there is one important message to consider, it's this: talent management is not only a process to integrate dozens of different HR and training practices—it is really a tool which helps your business leaders make better decisions and operate more effectively. Each and every business goal has a related people problem behind it—so think about your talent management process as a set of integrated tools which help business leaders rapidly address their own people and management needs. In our strategy and planning methodology, which we are happy to share with you, we focus very heavily on business strategy and business alignment before we advise organizations on their talent management approach.

Conclusion

Despite moderate satisfaction with their talent management systems, nearly 40 per cent of current users are not sure they want to renew their contracts and approximately one-third are dissatisfied with their current vendors. The recently published Talent Management Systems Customer Satisfaction 2010 highlights specific product, vendor, and implementation factors that drive customer success and satisfaction with these important corporate systems. The report also includes a section on how to use report findings in planning and selecting talent management systems. This special supplement is a companion to Talent Management Systems 2010, our comprehensive market review and buyer's guide for integrated talent management systems. This article helps in technology selection and implementation. Design a long-term architecture and plan, and develop a three- to five-year roadmap. Having established priorities for integration (by determining which processes create greatest business impact), you're now ready to design your long-term plan. Using a building block approach in developing your roadmap—one that defines the talent modules you'll integrate and implement first, second, and so on—will make certain that your organization attacks the most critical areas first.

REFERENCES

1. Conger, J. A., & Fulmer, R. M. (2003 *December). Developing Your Leadership Pipeline,* Harvard Business Review, 81(12).
2. Howard, A & Wellins, R. (2008). 23 Howard, A. & Wellins, R. (2008).
3. Howard, A. & Wellins, R. (2008). 15 *The Looming Leadership Void: Identifying, Developing and Retaining your Top Talent.* (2007 November). Aberdeen Group Research report available on line at ww.aberdeen.com.
4. Saba, J. & Martin, K. (2008 October). *Succession Management: Addressing the Leadership Development Challenge.* Howard, A. & Wellins, R. (2008). *Global Leadership Forecast 2008/ 2009.* Pittsburgh. PA: Development Dimensions International.
5. Teng, A. (May 2007). *Making the Business Case for MR: Talent Management aids Business Earnings.* HRO Today magazine. Retrieved from, http://www.hrotoday.com/Magazine.asp?art! D= 1693, on April 17, 2009.

CHAPTER

12

How Does an Organization Effective Talent Management

*Dr. H. Srinivasa Rao**

*Dr. R. N. Misra***

Talent Management

Talent Management professionals like us need good information and insight. It's the basis of good decision-making and risk management.

It takes Talent to spot Talent! A tone deaf will never be able to appreciate the music of maestros. Only a seasoned jeweller would know that all that glitters is not real! And, only those who can recognize the worth of a diamond can value it, for others it's just a stone! Talent is doing easily what others find difficult.

In an organization, there is nothing more crucial than fitting the right employee in the right position. Or else you would be trying to fit a square peg in a round hole. When people do jobs that just don't suit their liking, inclination or

*Sr. Lecturer in Commerce Badruka College of Commerce, Hyderabad, A.P.

**Prof. of Management Studies, SHIT, Berhampur, Orissa.

temperament, the results, or rather the lack of them, will be disastrously obvious. Low productivity, dissatisfaction, low morale, absenteeism and other negative behaviour will become typical till the employee is shown the door. Or perhaps, there is another option—Talent Management. Talent Management: A conscious, deliberate approach undertaken to attract, develop and retain people with the aptitude and abilities to meet current and future organizational needs. Talent management involves individual and organizational development in response to a changing and complex operating environment. It includes the creation and maintenance of a supportive, people oriented organization culture. Talent management implies recognizing a person's inherent skills, traits, personality and offering him a matching job. Every person has a unique talent that suits a particular job profile and any other position will cause discomfort.

It is the job of the Management, particularly the HR Department, to place candidates with prudence and caution. A wrong fit will result in further hiring, re-training and other wasteful activities.

No matter how inspiring the Leaders are, they are only as effective as their team. A team's output is healthy only if the members are in sync. To achieve such harmony, the key ingredient is "putting the right people in the right jobs".

While there is no magic formula to manage talent, the trick is to locate it and encourage it.

Talent Management is beneficial to both the organization and the employees. The organization benefits from: Increased productivity and capability; a better linkage between individuals' efforts and business goals; commitment of valued employees; reduced turnover; increased bench strength and a better fit between people's jobs and skills. Employees benefit from: Higher motivation and commitment; career development; increased knowledge about and contribution to company goals; sustained motivation and job satisfaction.

So, how does an organization effectively manage talent?

Recognise Talent: Notice what do employees do in their free time and find out their interests. Try to discover their strengths and interests. Also, encourage them to discover their own latent talents. For instance, if an employee in the operations department convincingly explains why he thinks he's right even when he's wrong, consider moving him to sales!

Attracting Talent: Good companies create a strong brand identity with their customers and then deliver on that promise. Great employment brands do the same, with quantifiable and qualitative results. As a result, the right people choose to join the organisation.

Selecting Talent: Management should implement proven talent selection systems and tools to create profiles of the right people based on the competencies of high performers. It's not simply a matter of finding the "best and the brightest" it's about creating the right fit—both for today and tomorrow.

Retaining Talent: In the current climate of change, it's critical to hold onto the key people. These are the people who will lead the organisation to future success, and you can't afford to lose them.

The cost of replacing a valued employee is enormous. Organizations need to promote diversity and design strategies to retain people, reward high performance and provide opportunities for development.

Managing Succession: Effective organisations anticipate the leadership and talent requirement to succeed in the future. Leaders understand that it's critical to strengthen their talent pool through succession planning, professional development, job rotation and workforce planning. They need to identify potential talent and groom it.

Change Organisation Culture: Ask yourself, "Why would a talented person choose to work here?" If the organisation wishes to substantially strengthen its talent pool, it should be prepared to change things as fundamental as the business strategy, the organisation structure, the culture and even the calibre of leaders in the organisation.

A rightly managed talent turns out to be a Gold Mine. It's inexhaustible and priceless. It will keep supplying wealth and value to the organisation.

In turn, Management needs to realise its worth, extract it, polish it and utilise it. Don't hoard Talent—spend it lavishly, like a millionaire flashing his luxuries, because Talent is Wealth!

Importance of Talent Management

Like human capital, Talent Management is gaining increased attention.

Talent Management (TM) brings together a number of important Human Resources (HR) and management initiatives.

Organisations that formally decide to "manage their talent" undertake a strategic analysis of their current HR processes. This is to ensure that a co-ordinated, performance oriented approach is adopted.

Quite often, organisations adopting a TM approach will focus on co-ordinating and integrating:

Recruitment—ensuring the right people are attracted to the organisation.

Retention—developing and implementing practices that reward and support employees.

Employee development—ensuring continuous informal and formal learning and development.

Leadership and "high potential employee" development—specific development programmes for existing and future leaders.

Performance management—specific processes that nurture and support performance, including feedback/ measurement.

Workforce planning—planning for business and general changes, including the older workforce and current/future skills shortages.

Culture—development of a positive, progressive and high performance "way of operating".

An important step is to identify the staff or employees (people and positions) that are critical to the organisation. They do not necessarily have to be senior staff members. Many organisations lost a lot of "organisational knowledge" in the downsizing exercises of a few years ago. The impact of the loss was not immediately apparent. However, it did not take long for many companies to realize their mistake when they did not have people with the knowledge and skills to either anticipate or solve problems that arose.

The current discussions about skill shortages and the ageing population are also helping organisations to focus on the talent management issue. It may not be possible to simply go out and recruit new people to meet operational needs. Many leading companies have decided to develop their own people, rather than trying to hire fully skilled workers.

In summary, every organisation should be implementing talent management principles and approaches.

Seven Talent Management Practices that Matter

Competing in a "flat world", a term popularized by columnist Tom Friedman, requires (well) rounded people. Becoming a well rounded talent requires continuous learning and development of knowledge and skills. Organizations that want to succeed in flat world competition better be creating enriching workplace experiences if they wish to attract and retain the high-caliber talent they need.

How can you create an enriching workplace? It isn't easy and doesn't happen overnight. But with some planning, a lot of persistence and adept execution of seven key practices, any organization can create an enriching workplace.

1. Job Stretch and Mobility

Feel like you're stuck in a box at work? If you do you've got plenty of company. Many organizations define jobs narrowly and allow little or no movement across organizational boundaries or even within them. But to grow, talented people need to be constantly challenged and stretched. This means the ability to take risks, to try new things, and yes, even to fail—whether by doing something differently in an existing job or tackling an entirely new one. If experience is indeed the best teacher how much are we learning if what we do rarely changes?

SEI Investments, a leading global provider of outsourced investment business solutions, has created an environment that provides continual challenge to staff and enables them to regularly move around the organization and to frequently take on new tasks and responsibilities.

2. Mentoring not Just Managing

Nothing speeds up the transfer of knowledge and know-how or enhances individual development more than a quality one-to-one dialogue between an experienced person and an up-and-comer.

W. L. Gore, creator of Gore-Tex fabrics, is a mentoring-intensive organization. Managers are called "Sponsors" and act as advocates for their assigned staff. They commit to being knowledgeable about their activities, well being, progress, accomplishments, personal concerns and ambitions. Each associate has at least one sponsor and some have more than one.

3. *Freedom and Stimulation*

Often the environment in which people work can make a huge difference to the speed and quality of people development. Two ingredients essential to making a workplace conducive to learning are stimulation—through frequent exposure to a wide variety people and ideas and the freedom to explore and pursue individual ideas and passions.

Google is a nirvana for the best and brightest technical talent in the world. The company's commitment to human capital is strong and was a core principle expressed in its now famous IPO filing in 2004. Staff are given huge amounts of freedom to determine when, where, how and on what they work. Each is allowed to spend 20 per cent of their time each week working on personally initiated projects.

4. *Deep Immersion*

Nothing frustrates talented people, particularly young up-and-comers, more than being asked to wait their turn before getting the opportunity to contribute to important projects or initiatives. This is not only demotivating to people but counter-productive to performance as opportunities to contribute depend more on tenure and pecking order than merit.

Trilogy, a software company based in Austin Texas not only avoids this problem, but has created a fast-track, merit-based process that starts with every new hire. Its induction programme is on steroids—goals are not only cultural induction, bonding and skill development but to create the company's next generation of ideas, products and leaders. The programme is led and run by Trilogy's top executives, including its CEO.

5. *Teaching and Coaching*

This means having people in the organization—both managers and specialists—whose role it is to help others to grow, learn and realize their potential. Many organizations have de-emphasized this key task as pressure to meet quarterly performance targets have cascaded down to every level of the organization.

Schools provide an inspiration and model from which other organizations can learn. They have teachers whose only job is to develop their student's skills and learning. While few organizations are positioned to employ full-time teachers, many should encourage and help managers and staff to take on this role. They can do this by explicitly acknowledging the value of teaching and coaching and including these responsibilities in the expectations and measures of performance set for managers and staff.

6. Diversity of Talents and Personalities

The value of diversity in business seems obvious to most observers, but few leaders really know how to leverage the differences that people bring to the workplace. As Ricardo Semler, head of the innovative Brazilian conglomerate Semco puts it—"I prefer Coq-au-Vin to Chicken McNuggets". He is not talking about food but rather cultures that blend diverse talents and perspectives (like the ingredients in a slow-cooked Coq-au-Vin) versus those that impose numbing conformity on their people (like the industrial-style sameness of Chicken McNuggets). And believe me, many companies have Chicken McNugget talent–mass produced, standardized and consistently mediocre. Far better to blend diverse ingredients into a rich and unique tasting stew - ala coq au vin!

Semco backs up its words with actions. It regularly pairs younger and older workers together. Its "Lost in Space" programme affords young staff the opportunity to move around the company on a regular basis during their first few years. This helps them to both develop new perspectives are well as inject their own fresh ideas throughout the business. Their "Trading Places" initiative let's people trade jobs as a way of gaining new experience and skills.

7. Horizontal Growth Paths

Flattening of hierarchies in recent years has severely curtailed growth paths in many organizations. But growth shouldn't just be up the ladder or depend purely on acquiring managerial skills. Another productive growth path is horizontal and progressive organizations have created lateral paths that allow people to broaden their skills and knowledge within their disciplines and jobs.

Companies like IBM, Texas Instruments and Intel have instituted technical mastery programmes to allow individual contributors and specialists to develop their knowledge and learning and to be paid and recognized for it. This means talent can advance based on their learning pace rather than have to change jobs or be promoted to get ahead.

Hype or Reality?

So how does your workplace stack up on these seven practices that matter most to creating an enriching workplace? Are job stretch and mobility, freedom and stimulation and horizontal growth paths the exception or the rule at your employer? Are mentoring, teaching and coaching rare or pervasive throughout your organization? Is diversity merely an overused word in your company's communications or a real principle on which your organization operates every day?

Targeted Talent Management Source: Unknown

Most large organizations talk about Talent Management as part of their wider strategy. It is a crucial way of securing, developing and motivating people with the right skills and approaches to meet business objectives. But how many of our strategic goals are fully met by our talented people? All too often, we find that we don't have the right people in place to fill a gap when it appears, or we simply can't keep hold of the individuals we want. Even worse, talented people may simply not be operating at the levels we require. So what can we do to seize these missed opportunities? I believe that the biggest single challenge is achieving genuine "connectedness" between Talent Strategy and Business Strategy. A wide range of people processes often take place without a clear relationship with the ultimate aims and culture of the business.

Think about recruitment, performance management and development—to what extent are these processes based on a clear analysis of the talents and skills that people will need to operate at the next level? To what extent do you build people's capability and motivation to meet the needs of the business in a few years' time? It is vitally important to build a clear definition of what each organisation really means by talent throughout the organisation. The acid test is simple—do people with these qualities deliver the kinds of business success we are aiming for?

In a project that I am involved with at the moment, I am working with a major organisation that has a very clear sense of its future strategic direction. It is investing now in its people by providing feedback and coaching—targeting not only each person's natural areas of strength, but also pinpointing the specific qualities that the organisation will need in the future. Crucially, this is not a one-hit wonder—the outcomes are linked to how people are managed, developed and motivated. The direct effect on business outcomes will be tracked and analysed. It is this joined-up quality that makes a significant difference—linking business strategy to people's daily experience of the organisation.

It is vitally important that individual aspirations and organisational goals are delivered together. Too often, these are seen as unequal partners. However, organisations that genuinely focus on understanding each person's own natural talents tend to achieve corporate success. We need to create different routes for people to progress and develop; otherwise we will only appeal to a narrow range of people. This approach requires an open mind, tackling questions like "How can we use this person's talents and energies?", "How can we organise our work differently?" or "Are we aiming for the wrong things?" But if such issues are genuinely addressed, great things can be achieved.

"Alignment" is another key element of a successful Talent Strategy. When selecting or developing people, most organisations focus on the skills, knowledge, experience and behaviours required for the role. However, some organisations are beginning to look at the behaviours required to operate effectively in a particular team or culture. Working with Professors Michael West and Neil Anderson, ASE have an approach that looks at all of the factors that drive team performance (not simply the "types" of people in the team), and this leads to impressive results. We need to understand the relationship between people's motivations and the sorts of organisational cultures in which they will thrive.

Talent Management should be about delivering business success through understanding what we actually mean by talent, and how it will achieve the specific goals of the organisation. It is about ensuring that we value the natural talents and aspirations of our people. It is about ensuring that we understand what blockages can spoil all our hard work, it is about operating people processes that join together not only with each other, but with the business's goals. And finally, it is also about understanding how to manage people for alignment as well as ability. If we adopt these approaches, not only will business success follow, but we should also have fulfilled and effective people.

Index

N

P

R

S

T